Agile Distribution®
Application of Lean Principles

Dr. Perry Daneshgari

ISBN: 10: 1978279760
ISBN-13: 978-1978279766

Copyright ©. 2008-2017 Dr. Perry Daneshgari

First Published by NAW Institute for Distribution Excellence in 2008

MCA Inc.
363 East Grand Blanc Road,
Grand Blanc, Michigan 48439
(810) 232-9797
www.mca.net
www.mca-soft.com

CONTENTS

FOREWORD

Progressive wholesaler-distributors continually optimize their operations by cutting unnecessary costs and reducing waste. Toyota, a world leader in automobile manufacturing, pioneered work on a business improvement process now called "lean." The vast majority of books written on this subject to date are drawn from the experience of Toyota and other manufacturers that have successfully applied lean principals to their business processes. In those cases in which the lean improvement process has been fully implemented, success has most often been stunning.

While these books are educational in understanding the principles of lean, very little is currently written about how to apply lean principles to distribution. With the publication of this book we hope to initiate interest in this vital subject of wholesaler-distributors.

Author Dr. Perry Daneshgari has taken the lessons learned in other industries that have adopted lean principles and applied them to wholesaler-distributors in a systematic way that promotes a clear understanding of lean and how distributors can really benefit by applying lean concepts to their operation.

As Dr. Perry reminds us, applying lean principles to your business is a journey, not a destination. Lean will help you look at and improve every business process within your wholesale distribution company. And, lean is about improving these processes over and over again. Continuous improvement is at the core of what it means to "go lean."

If your company hasn't yet embarked on a lean journey, then this book can provide you with the foundation for understanding lean and offer you a starting point for discussion with your top management. This book will show you what the lean implementation process is, and what the tools are that you can use to measure, monitor and evaluate your existing systems for continuous improvement. What's most helpful is that this book includes real-world examples—stories from a local distributor, a regional distributor, and a national distributor—and walks you through the steps that each took in implementing a lean strategy that led to improvements in their operations.

I encourage you to use this book to start your lean journey. Provide copies to your management team and begin reading and learning together to see how these principles can be applied to your business. To start the journey will require the full support of your company's management team, starting with you. I wish you great success in creating your lean implementation strategy, a process that will improve your performance, cut waste, reduce cost, eliminate errors, and better serve your customers!

Byron Potter
Chairman
NAW Institute for Distribution Excellence

ACKNOWLEDGMENTS
Second Edition

Much has happened since the publication of the first "Lean Distribution" book. Our work with tens of distributors on the application of Agile Distribution® and Lean processes has taken us from one side of the country to the other. Companies which have successfully applied the lessons learned from many other industries especially from manufacturing and automotive have benefited from higher margins and market share. Distributors such as Graybar, under the leadership of Bob Reynolds and currently Kathy Mazzarella as well as Steve Stone; Mayer Electric Supply under the leadership of Nancy Collat Goedecke and Wes Smith; ConneXion under the leadership of David Rosenstein and Steve Abrams, Werner Electric Supply under the leadership of Scott Teerlinck and Terry MacDonald; North Coast Electric in Seattle, and tens of other suppliers have been able to use these principles and create a new ecosystem for the distribution industry. Their value transfer to their clients has gone from just supplying parts to managing information and total integration management. They are no longer just a bystander but rather part of the total delivery system to the final assembly line.

We here at MCA Inc. have also learned much from working with these great companies. I am humbled by leaders of the distribution companies, whom have applied these principles, their visions and ability to form the future. Our team's ability has grown by applying the scientific principles of process design, learned from manufacturing and automotive in the distribution industry.

Dr. Heather Moore is now second to none in the entire industry in application of Agile and Lean principals. Sonja Daneshgari our Field Operations Manager, Phil Nimmo our VP of Business Development, Michelle Wilson our Research and Development scientist and the rest of our team has made it possible to pass on many lessons learned and applications throughout the industry. Naturally, our backbone of operations Ms. Anna VanWagner is our Rock of Gibraltar. I also need to acknowledge our teams' personal pillars, their spouses and family members who make it possible for our team to do their work. Specifically, David Moore, Heather's husband; and my wife Jennifer, who have walked alongside us on this journey.

I am truly amazed, humbled and thankful for all the help I have received to "Make a Dent in The Universe". As Sir Isaac Newton well said; to achieve anything in life we need to "stand on the shoulders of giants", who have come before us and have helped us to connect the dots. I am forever grateful for the men and women before us to give us the gift of knowledge and my team to help me put it in place.

Enjoy your journey,

Dr. Perry (Parviz) Daneshgari
October 3, 2017
Grand Blanc, Michigan

ACKNOWLEDGMENTS
First Edition

This is the hardest part of any publication for me; how do I go about acknowledging all the people who have contributed to me becoming me? Do I start with my kindergarten teacher? Well I could, but I never went to kindergarten. **Perhaps I should start with my university professors, as I attended many schools over a period of 30 years.** Do I start with all of my mentors, such as Dr. W. E. Deming, Dr. Peter Drucker, Jim Swartz, Tom Stephens, my brother Dr. Firouz Daneshgari, my wife Jennifer Daneshgari, Robert Reynolds, Robert Bruce, Jay Bruce, Charles and Charlie Colette, Jim Summerline, Wes Smith, and Glenn Goedecke. That won't work either; I have had too many mentors. Maybe I should start by going backwards and just give up when the list gets to be too long. Okay, I will do that.

Naturally, the most important acknowledgments go to the Board of Directors of the NAW Institute for Distribution Excellence, since without its approval there would be no book.

Without the help of my companions, co-workers, and friends at MCA, Inc., I would not have had a prayer in collecting, compiling, analyzing, and presenting this work. Here, too, I don't know where to start.

Dr. Heather Moore started 5 years ago as a co-op student with me. Most, if not all, of the data, measurements, illustrations, and analysis are her work. I am not sure how I got lucky in having such a genius work with me. She will be the next Dr. Deming for this industry. Naturally, you will see Michelle Wilson's work in this book and there is not much I can add. However, it is her tenacity and hard work decoding and analyzing data and applications that brings the intangible ideas to the tangible world. Her keen eye for translating dry statistics to real-life applications is unmatched by anyone I know.

Phil Nimmo conducted many of the onsite implementations of lean application in the distribution industry. His work over the past 18 years has helped companies to realize millions of dollars in profitability. After working with Phil, one small distributor in California increased profits by 70% within a year. Phil's contribution can be seen throughout the book.

Anna VanWagner's patient work and follow-up kept all the appointments and dates on time. She has worked with me for more than 7 years and has not missed a beat keeping me on task.

Of course, your readers are the most important part of this equation; without you there will be no application. So, relax, read, and execute.

INTRODUCTION

Seldom do we pause and think about the world around us in the way we think about our daily activities. How did McDonald's develop the fast food industry? What made us trust flying airplanes? Why do we trust that the milk we buy from the grocery store is drinkable? What would happen if the insurance companies could not insure our international mercantile exchange? Why are cell phones so widely used? Did we not have as much to talk about before the cell phone?

All of the tangible things around us have had a chance to go through design, development, prototyping, production, and implementation stages. But our processes don't get the same chance; we don't think they need to be designed. This book is about that. It is about how we can make our intangible surroundings become visible and manageable so that we can, in turn, continuously improve them. This book is about creating lean operations in wholesale distribution--a culture focused on eliminating waste, reducing errors, and adding value.

The good thing about lean is that, like all business principles, it follows the laws of nature—that is, just as natural laws (for example, the law of gravity) have no boundaries and apply universally, so do the laws of lean. This way of thinking helps break down barriers to lean by showing that it's not specific to certain industries and can (and indeed, should) be applied in wholesale distribution. This means that if we are able to develop principles that apply across all industries, then specific models can be developed that are unique to each industry. In this book, you will see a translation of business and lean models applied to wholesale distribution.

Once I was asked the very direct question, *"Does lean apply to the distribution industry?"* having had much success applying business and lean principles across various industries, my answer was a very clear "yes." The distribution industry has always tried to be at the leading edge of technological innovation. However, technology, at best, will keep an industry at par with national averages. To excel and exceed national averages, the application of technology must be supplemented with innovation in processes—that is, with the application of business and lean principles.

Applying lean concepts makes sense because becoming lean means becoming a more effective company—one that operates with minimal waste and few errors, with maximized value transferred to the products and services it provides. For wholesaler-distributors, becoming lean means continually improving the way you process orders and serve customers—from the time you seek an order, to order entry, and all the way through to delivery of products and services. This book deals specifically with those operations.

It's important to know that lean is not a destination; it is a journey. And few companies embark on this journey alone. Just like a surgeon cannot perform surgery on himself, neither can a distributor evaluate and improve his systems all on his own. Outside expertise—in the form of consultants, training courses, and the like—go hand in hand with implementing a lean strategy. The purpose of this book is to introduce wholesaler-distributors to lean concepts and show how other distributors have used those concepts to improve their businesses. This book provides a foundation for understanding lean and offers a starting point for distributors of all sizes.

Lean: Reshaping the Business Landscape

It was not that long ago that the United States, with the help of the Marshall Plan, helped rebuild the nations that were in ruins after World War II. Japan was one nation that benefited from American management and technological know-how. For example, the first Honda motorcycles were built on Harley Davidson's tools; the first Toyota passenger car had a Chevy engine. When I started my research on the differences between Toyota and General Motors back in 1989, I did not expect to discover basic universal business operational principles that would apply across all industries. At the time, Toyota was 10 times more profitable than its counterparts in the United States. Since then, major strides toward improving productivity and profitability by American automobile manufacturers have improved that industry's productivity more than two-fold.

Going back even further, Fredrick Taylor's 1911 work, *The Principles of Scientific Management*, was the first published literature to hint at better ways of managing resources. Taylor recognized that "maximum prosperity can exist only as the result of maximum productivity" (p. 12). The productivity he sought came through redirecting the "…awkward, inefficient, or ill-directed movements of men" (p. 5) into productive, value-adding activity. At that time, Taylor could not possibly have imagined the impact and longevity of his work.

In the last three decades, Taylor's principles, now commonly called "lean," have been applied in many industries around the world. What's more, by applying lean operating principles, many of these industries have contributed to growth in

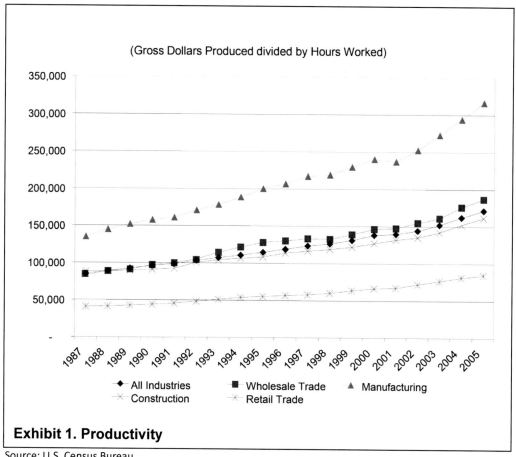

Exhibit 1. Productivity

Source: U.S. Census Bureau

national prosperity—a direct result of increased productivity. Reduced inventories, the end of the Cold War, and the application of Taylor's work have catapulted national productivity to levels that were unimaginable just a few years ago.

Government census data indicate that productivity is increasing throughout the United States. Productivity in manufacturing alone has increased more than 180% in the last 50 years. Trends indicate that the wholesale distribution industry leads in terms of overall productivity when compared to other industries that have not yet successfully applied lean principles, such as construction and retail trade. However, when compared to industries that have applied lean principles—such as manufacturing—the wholesale distribution industry lags behind (exhibit I). Manufacturing has more than doubled its productivity rate in the past 20 years while growth in wholesale distribution has increased more than 57% during the same time frame.

Regardless of the industry, the effects of implementing lean speak for themselves:

- A regional bank in Michigan reduced the time required for producing a small business loan from 3 to 5 weeks to less than 2.6 hours. Simultaneously, the cost to produce the loans dropped to half while the number of loans produced increased five times by 20% fewer people.
- An electrical distributor in Atlanta increased its warehouse capacity for picking lines by better than 40% through the application of lean warehouse processes and increased its profits by more than five times.
- A computer manufacturer in Michigan reduced its production time for delivery of a customized individual computer from 2 weeks down to only 2 hours using a lean, customer-driven "build-to-ship" philosophy.
- A large equipment manufacturer now operates with a buffer of no more than 4 days of finished-goods inventory after applying lean principles throughout its production facilities.
- A construction subcontractor in California increased its annual sales volume from $15 million to $50 million within 3 years, while simultaneously increasing net profits from 1.5% to 11% through the application of Strategic Breakthrough Process Improvement (SBPI®, which will be explained in chapter 4).

- An internationally renowned medical facility in Ohio applied SBPI® to its research funding processes and in less than 1year was able to triple its hit ratio (grants applied for to grants received) for government-sponsored medical research.

Practicing Lean

Since the introduction of management science, which is primarily credited to Dr. Peter Drucker, the "buzzword jungle" has been one of the byproducts of the application of effective production and management processes. Dr. Deming, the founder of the new age of quality in processing and production, would be the first to question popular terminology such as "Total Quality Management" or "TQM." Today, we hear the terminology of lean, in English as well as other languages, being used without a full understanding of underlying principles.

The fact is, the basic principles remain the same no matter what they are called. We don't have to borrow from a foreign language to express our desire to apply better science of management to our resources. My assumption is that you, as the readers of this book, know your businesses. You are reading because you have recognized a gap between your operational performance and your strategic plan and are now seeking solutions. To that end, no tools or terminology can replace your understanding of lean concepts. This book focuses on the principles and their application; it is not an "owner's manual" for a lean operation. The owner's manual can only be developed as the distributor applies the principles to its own unique model.

From the automotive industry to banking, construction, distribution, retailing, insurance, and health care, lean principles and applications have helped hundreds of companies surpass their competitors. My work with more than 300 companies—and their continuous success—is evidence that applying lean and business principles works. Your journey will start with this book and continue with constant challenges and the exhilaration in discovering higher productivity, quality, and lower cost. Like every journey, the toughest part is the first step. If you would like to discover what you can do with your resources and get them to produce at an unimaginable rate, read on.

EXECUTIVE SUMMARY

Almost everything around us—everything we see, touch and use—has been designed and developed by people. And it's all been designed to be used in a specific way. We expect a car to provide transportation, and it does exactly that. We expect a clock to keep time, and it keeps time. We understand that human intervention makes these things possible; we know that without us, none of it would work. But when it comes to business processes—the steps necessary to design, build, and distribute the things we see and use every day—we often expect them to happen by themselves.

This is where lean principles can help. Lean and an optimized supply chain begin with well-designed processes driven by customers' buying and usage habits. Each process starts with the customer and works back through the entire channel to provide the lowest usage cost to the customer and the highest profits to channel members. Lean doesn't happen by itself; it happens by design. And the design phase begins by optimizing the wholesaler-distributor's operations from the customer's perspective, then optimizing the rest of the channel from the same perspective.

This book examines lessons learned in other industries as they underwent the transformation to lean and applies those lessons to wholesale distribution. It discusses the steps a wholesaler-distributor must take to design and manage a lean culture. Specifically, it deals with a lucrative area for distributors: operations, which includes all aspects of the order processing system--from warehousing to order production to delivery.

Chapters 1 through 4 lay the groundwork, explaining what lean is, why it is important, and how distributors can apply lean strategies in their businesses. Chapters 5 through 7 present case studies of companies that have used lean strategies to improve operations. Additional sources of information are included in the appendices, glossary, and references and resources at the end of the book.

Also included for your reference are the results of an exclusive survey conducted by the NAW Institute for Distribution Excellence and MCA, Inc. specifically for this book (chapter 8). We surveyed wholesaler-distributors to gauge their familiarity with lean and to measure some key performance indicators for the industry as a whole.

At a glance, this book offers:

Chapter 1

This chapter answers the question: *What is lean?*

At its core, lean is about continuous improvement; it's about striving to improve all aspects of your business—every process you adhere to, every procedure you undertake. This involves eliminating waste in your company, reducing errors, and thereby adding value to the products and services you, as a distributor, provide. Chapter 1 lays the groundwork for lean by introducing the fundamental principles of System Design, Team Technology, and Process Models used to create a lean culture.

Chapter 2

This chapter answers the question: *Why is lean important?*

Lean is important because it helps you become a better-run distribution company by eliminating waste, reducing errors, and adding value. But lean is not a one-time application of processes and procedures. The core focus on value, quality, and flow must be fully part of your company culture. Furthermore, a lean wholesaler-distributor requires a lean philosophy of operation that starts at the top with the board of directors and is carried all the way down and across the company. Chapter 2 emphasizes four key elements to a lean strategy: value, quality, process flow, and lean operations.

Chapter 3

This chapter answers the question: *Why should I pursue lean?*

In its simplest form, a lean process can be described as doing the right things (no waste) in the right way (no errors), so the opportunities come in two primary forms:

- Reducing and eliminating waste
- Reducing and eliminating errors

These two objectives clear the way to adding value, which is your primary goal as a wholesaler-distributor. Chapter 3 discusses the nature and impact of waste and errors in wholesale distribution and describes some of the key measurements and tools distributors can use to pursue lean.

Chapter 4

This chapter answers the question: *"How do you apply lean?"*

It describes the lean implementation process, focusing on some of the tools that can be used to measure, monitor, and evaluate your existing systems for continuous improvement. In particular, it discusses in detail the Strategic Breakthrough Process Improvement method, which is a strategy for implementing lean in a wholesale distribution company.

Chapters 5, 6, and 7

This portion of the book deals with real-world examples. Chapter 5 is a case study of how a national distributor implemented lean to improve operations. Chapter 6 examines a regional distributor's lean strategy. Chapter 7 is a case study of how a local distributor implemented lean.

Chapter 8

This section examines the results of a survey conducted by the NAW Institute for Distribution Excellence and MCA, Inc. The survey gauged wholesaler-distributors' understanding of lean and set out to answer these questions:

- What is the status of lean in the wholesale distribution industry today?
- Do distributors understand lean concepts?
- Do they use lean concepts and principles to measure their performance and make improvements to their operations?
- Could the wholesale distribution industry really benefit from implementing lean?

CHAPTER 1

What Is Lean?

The following statement can't be overemphasized: Lean is a journey, not a destination. At its core, lean is about continuous improvement; it's about striving to improve all aspects of your business—every process you adhere to, every procedure you undertake. This involves eliminating waste in your company, reducing errors, and thereby adding value to the products and services you, as a distributor, provide.

To that end, distributors can never truly "become" lean. Rather, the point is to continually strive to create a leaner organization focused on delivering the highest quality products and services at the lowest possible operating cost. Of course, this is easier said than done. Lean is a discipline that requires a cultural shift on the part of the distributor, a new way of thinking about how to run the business, and an education on the methods and tools used to implement a lean philosophy.

The first step is to instill a lean culture. This starts at the top and works its way down and across the wholesale distribution company. Top executives must embrace lean thinking and then get the rest of the employees to embrace it as well. The number one enemy of lean is the anxiety it causes at the onset of application. More than 70% of attempted Business Process Reengineering applications (the predecessor to lean) failed due to the lack of support and inclusion of the "do-er bees"—the ones who must think it, live it, and implement it on a daily basis.

So how do you get buy-in from employees? First of all, involve them in the process. Explain that lean is not about eliminating jobs, it is about becoming a better-run distributor. It's about continuously improving their daily tasks in order to deliver the right products and services to the right customers at the right time—every time. Explain that this can't possibly happen without them. Indeed, lean is not about eliminating people; it is about engaging people and focusing on their ability to continuously improve what they do.

To focus on that, this book deals with a lucrative area for distributors—operations, which includes order processing, warehousing, and delivery. The following framework for understanding lean principles addresses the subject from that perspective, focusing on how distributors can improve operations and reduce operating costs.

Getting Started

Lean industries embrace fundamental organizational principles. In wholesale distribution, the importance of these principles is underscored by the fact that a distributor cannot pursue lean unless the entire company adopts a lean operating philosophy and develops a structure to support it. Similarly, the supply chain as a whole can't pursue lean unless these principles are recognized and applied throughout the chain. Although lean principles are universal and apply across all industries—from manufacturing to construction to wholesale distribution—their implementation varies. In other words, particular application models are specific to both the industry and the company. Sample models used for applying lean in wholesale distribution are described in chapters 3 and 4.

Simply put, lean organizational principles allow distributors to improve productivity and reduce costs. These principles must be thoroughly understood in order to build a structure that will support lean operations in wholesale distribution and throughout the supply chain.

The principles can be organized into five major categories:

1. System Design
2. Team Technology
3. Process Models
4. Organizational Learning
5. Methods and Tools.

System Design, Team Technology and Process Models are described in this chapter because they deal with the practical aspects of adopting a lean philosophy and developing a lean culture. The more theoretical concepts of Organizational Learning and Methods and Tools are discussed in appendix A.

System Design

System design principles have to do with the efficiency of the entire distribution company. The underlying philosophy behind design in a lean organization is "synthesis"—designing a system that allows the departments and functions within the wholesaler-distributor to smoothly integrate. In a lean organization, the improvements you make to each aspect of the system must improve the system entirely. In other words, the whole will be improved by "improving the whole." The entire system has to be optimized.

Discontinuities, such as those that occur in the handoff from sales to operations—or even those that occur within a single process—are often the biggest culprits, causing waste and higher costs. Discontinuities most often occur at transitions and points of interface between two departments or business processes.

 As an example, consider the inherent difference in the structure, style, compensation, and functions of your sales and operations departments. Many distributors concentrate their system improvement efforts in either sales or operations based on each department's needs rather than focusing on the entire system. This approach actually increases waste since it does nothing to ensure disturbance-free "change points" within the company.

No business process exists in a vacuum; that's why it's important to take a big-picture approach to system design. As a case in point: A study at one wholesaler-distributor identified its 10 most costly causes of non-productive time during picking in a warehouse as

1. Walking or driving
2. Looking for material
3. Getting or using equipment to move material
4. Transferring material from one location to another
5. Determining which location to go to next/which item to pull next
6. Scanning or verifying material

7. Waiting—for instructions or for tickets to print
8. Sorting material and breaking down packaging
9. Talking
10. Moving equipment or material out of the way.

Of these items, only number 5, "determining which item to pull next," is specifically a picking activity—and even that is more strongly affected by warehouse design than by the picking process itself. A perfectly designed picking process without an adequate supporting structure is not unlike purchasing an F16 fighter plane with only 3,000 feet of runway available at the take-off airport. There is no use for the perfect flying machine without the appropriate support structure. Similarly, without attention to the system in which the picking process operates, the perfect picking process will still function within the same system that required it to include the non-productive activities in the first place.

There are two key elements of system design:

- Processes and procedures
- Value delivery.

Processes and Procedures

Processes and procedures exist in all wholesale distribution companies. They may be defined, documented, visible, and agreed upon, or they may simply evolve as a part of the prevailing culture. Well-defined processes streamline the relationships between functional areas of the organization and the individuals carrying out the activities of business.

A "procedure" is a series of activities conducted to complete a process. Procedures offer the operational "how-to" to accomplish a particular task. For example, receiving material is one procedure under the order processing system. Opening receiving bays, unloading trucks, and verifying material are a few of the activities that make up the receiving procedure. A procedure concentrates on the correctness of the step and tries to improve the individual efficiency of its occurrences.

A "process" is the collection of steps and procedures that leads to an expected outcome (GM Power Train, 1991). A process constantly questions the necessity of every step and works on the effectiveness of the series of events. A process raises questions such as "Why are we doing this?" and "Where does this add value?" and will be self-correcting when the answers are not satisfactory.

A process must start with an objective goal and end with a deliverable outcome. One example is the order processing system noted above. With a final objective of filling sales orders with the correct material for delivery to the correct customer as and how requested, this process begins with receiving material into the warehouse. The process continues with stocking the material, picking a ticket, verifying the correct material was pulled, packing the material, and loading the trucks, and ends with a transition to the customer—this includes the driver or trucking company responsible for final delivery of material to the end user (exhibit 1-1).

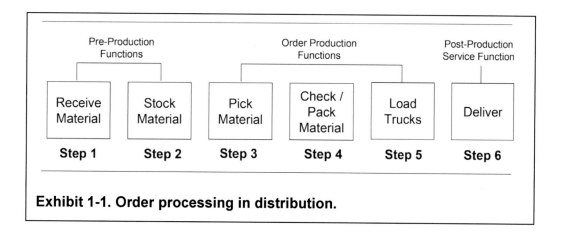

Exhibit 1-1. Order processing in distribution.

This process illustrates the major characteristics of any process:

- A clear objective (internal material management, in this case)
- A clear deliverable (the fulfillment of the order)
- A defined end (the transition to the delivery process).

Depending on the organizational structure of the company, the distinction between process and procedure is sometimes unclear. One company may have a formal purchase order process and another may have only procedures that dictate how to process purchase orders. The procedures concentrate on the correctness of each of the individual processing steps without looking at the total cost of processing the purchase order. A procedure's steps do not require validation; a company may have a perfectly executed system for processing purchase orders yet not even need the purchase orders. A process, on the other hand, will raise questions such as:

- Do we need this many purchase orders?
- Can we work with one purchase order per vendor?
- Can we use other mechanisms, such as electronic data interchange (EDI)?

To put it simply, a procedure focuses on "doing the things right," whereas a process addresses "doing the right things." Correct procedure improves efficiency and correct process improves effectiveness. As wholesaler-distributors, you need to do both things well, with an eye toward adding value for the customer. When your typical purchase order costs $72 per order to process internally, directing the entire effort to value-added activity is essential.

Value Delivery: Valueless Time, Valueless Variance, and Valueless Activity

Applying system design principles leads to faster response, higher quality, and lower cost of delivering goods and services. Better time, cost, and quality translate into higher value and higher value-to-cost ratios for the customer.

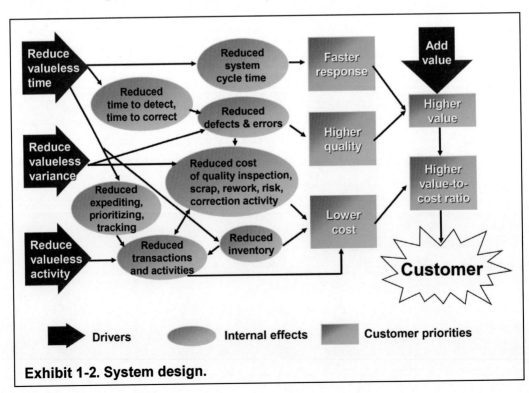

Exhibit 1-2. System design.

Exhibit 1-2 is a value stream map that illustrates the main drivers impacting the value delivery process: valueless time, valueless variance, and valueless activity. "Value stream mapping" is a lean technique used to analyze the flow of materials and information required to bring a product or service to a customer. (See the glossary for more about information value stream mapping). By designing processes that reduce the impact of these three value impediments—which are the main contributors to waste—the time, cost, and quality of order processing will improve and the system can be optimized.

Valueless Time: Valueless time in wholesale distribution companies is any time spent on activities that prolong either or both of the following:

- **System Cycle Time:** The time needed to produce any order, from the time of initial order to the time of final delivery.
- **Time to Detect and Time to Correct:** The time from the discovery of a problem to the resolution of all its issues.

Valueless time also includes time spent on expediting, prioritizing, and tracking, which increases not only the cycle time of a particular transaction, but often the overall number of transactions and other related activities as well.

Valueless Variance: Valueless variance is the inconsistency introduced into your system by a locally optimized process flow design—that is, a process flow that tries to correct one department often at the expense of another.

For wholesaler-distributors, valueless variance increases operating costs by adding the cost of quality inspection that a well-designed process would render unnecessary. For example, an invisible and complex quotation process, fully understood by only the most experienced salespeople, has considerable valueless variation. Where an experienced salesperson may fully document an order that he expects to convert, including tax status, delivery instructions, related freight charge estimates, and so on, a less experienced salesperson may note fewer details or use a non-specific format. As each new salesperson gains experience, he develops his own methods of producing quotes until he can produce a complete, repeatable quote. In this example, the variation could be avoided entirely by creating a process that recognizes and captures the components necessary for converting a quote into an order, fully avoiding rework and corrective activities.

Valueless Activities: Valueless activities are activities introduced into your system that are unnatural to the process flow, increasing transactions without providing additional value to the final product or service.

For example, using a cart during the picking process may facilitate the organization and preparation of an order, but locating an empty or unused cart and moving it to the beginning of a picking run adds no value to the items being picked. If instead the cart could be used to transport returned items on its way back to the beginning of the picking process, this valueless activity can become a value-added activity.

By reducing valueless time, variation, and activities, your products and services will cost less, have higher quality, and you will be able to turn them around faster. Simultaneously, fewer defects and errors will result in less rework, fewer corrective activities, and fewer transactions.

What's more, exhibit 1-2 illustrates the higher value the customer receives when you reduce (or improve upon) valueless time, variance, and activities (Swartz, 1994). Keep in mind that the wholesale distribution system can only add value to customers if it is designed from their perspective and with their needs in mind. System design principles and lean processes will streamline value production throughout the entire distributorship only when applied according customers' needs.

Team Technology

The increasing complexities of today's work environment and technical know-how have forced many distributors to divide work by specialty area. However, specialization results in reduced information flow within and between departments. In addition, any time information is exchanged between departments, a discontinuity, or break, exists, potentially allowing the entrance of misinformation or missing information. At this transfer point, the gap also forces an unwanted disturbance in the quality of work performed, even if the quality of the product is maintained.

For example, the workflow in your sales department is very different from the workflow at your order processing or delivery phases. The salesperson may not need specific delivery instructions—such as "call the following number 15 minutes before arrival so that the gate is unlocked"—in order to process a sales order, yet the driver needs that information to complete his task. Since the salesperson may not consider this information essential, it may be overlooked or omitted, requiring unwanted extra steps in the delivery phase—in the form of rework by recontacting the customer for the information, or in the form of waste by having to wait additional time or even make a second delivery trip to ultimately process the order. This is where "information throughput" becomes crucial. Information throughput is defined by communication bandwidth. Bandwidth refers to the amount of information that is intact from the beginning to the end of your business process. The wider the bandwidth, the better the communication and the higher the quality of information flow. Information throughput is a direct result of interdepartmental communication. The weaker the

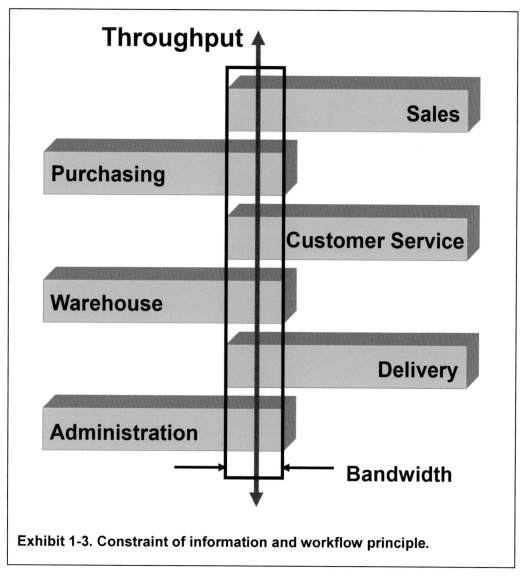

Exhibit 1-3. Constraint of information and workflow principle.

communication process, the less information will be sent through the organization and vice versa.

Constraints and bottlenecks in your business system limit bandwidth and restrict information flow. Identifying the amount of correct, usable information that arrives at the end of the process can help you measure the bandwidth of your company's throughput. In other words, it will show how much information is actually being shared between and among departments. Exhibit 1-3 illustrates these concepts for the departments of a wholesale distribution company.

Increasing communication bandwidth within your company helps improve the quality of information that is carried through the organization—especially as it relates to value-added activities such as fulfilling an order. A wider bandwidth occurs when there is more interaction between and among departments and when that interaction is focused on the common goal of servicing the customer. More information is carried through and shared as the value-added activity proceeds through the stages to completion. Communication that occurs outside the bandwidth may not be essential to the completion of the activity, but has developed out of necessity to meet the needs of a particular department.

Consider a small distributorship where the owner can do everything himself. He has complete knowledge of all operations and doesn't need to explain anything to anyone. However, as his sales volume increases, he needs to add more people: a warehouse manager, salespeople, material buyers, and so forth. The information no longer flows as smoothly as before. The profits per order are decreasing. With increased help he earns less money on each dollar sold. In order to return the productivity and profitability to the small-shop level, the organization needs to regain the complete knowledge that the owner possessed when the distributorship was small. The lean approach ultimately tries to return the overall operation of the company to the original state of one mind/one mission.

The workflow and structure between the elements of the wholesaler-distributor, or of the entire supply chain, strongly affect the "leaning" of the organization. Inefficient transfer of information, products or services means that work is being done to complete activities that cannot add value to the customer or result in profits to the company.

Using "team technology"—in which a cross-functional team of employees works closely together—distributors can create a seamless workflow between and among departments in which information is transferred fully intact. The specialized knowledge and experience of a cross-functional team can increase the bandwidth of information flow, with a resulting increase in capability and capacity. However, to do so, the team must

- understand the company's core competencies
- identify the specialties needed to deliver the core competencies
- understand the workflow requirements of each department
- identify the workflow and information-flow bandwidth
- increase the capability of the entire system.

Most importantly, the cross-functional team must be driven to optimize the workflow from the customer's perspective.

Process Models: Visibility of Systems and Processes

Finally, visible process models (or diagrams) allow you to put all of this together, so you can understand your workflow, production requirements, and the interactions between and among the various roles and departments as they currently exist. In addition to measuring quality and value, visible systems allow you to measure and understand your costs in order to more effectively manage operational efficiencies and profitability.

Processes, by nature, are intangible. In a lean system, process models must clearly illustrate the value delivered to the customer and make it visible throughout the system. Distributors can then use the models to examine logic, waste, and valueless activities. How do you create these models? By using a tool called "mapping," which allows you to identify the areas that require change or present opportunities for improvement The value stream map described earlier in this chapter is an example of one kind of mapping technique. Mapping will be discussed in more detail in chapters 3 and 4.

The next chapter discusses why lean is important for your company, pointing to the four key elements of a lean system: Lean Operations, Value, Quality, and Process Flow.

CHAPTER 2

Why Is Lean Important?

Lean is important because it helps you become a better-run distribution company by eliminating waste, reducing errors, and adding value. But lean is not a one-time application of processes and procedures. The core focus on value, quality, and flow must be fully part of your company's culture. As stated earlier, a lean wholesaler-distributor requires a lean philosophy of operation that starts at the top with the board of directors and is carried all the way down through the organization. The entire structure must support the underlying lean principles of

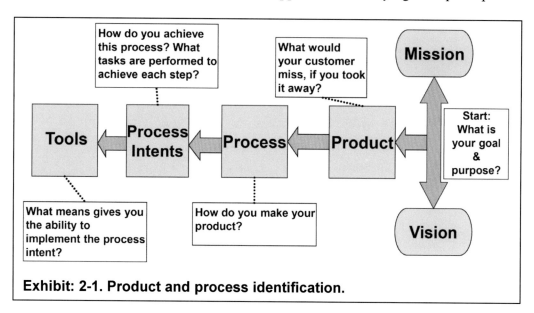

Exhibit: 2-1. Product and process identification.

focusing on customers' needs while reducing waste and rework.

Furthermore, a lean distributor begins with a pragmatic vision and mission: What the company is, where it will be, and a strategic plan for how to get there, as shown in exhibit 2-1. (This exhibit must be read from right to left, indicating the distributor's response to customer input.)

The operational philosophy of having the broadest selection, lowest price, best service, friendliest atmosphere, and being the most reliable drives your product and service offerings. This philosophy establishes the performance differences between competing companies. That, in turn, drives customers' perception of the value they receive from each distributor. Often, this operational philosophy is the only thing that distinguishes you from your competitors, as the products and services within your industry may be comparable.

Your process of production (the system you use to process orders) must then be designed to support and deliver those products and services efficiently. This process must integrate all departments and functions that directly or indirectly participate in processing your products and services. Once the process is designed to support lean operations, you can select the technology to support it.

The luxury of starting a company with a clean sheet of paper is rare. Established organizations must become lean in spite of ongoing operations and existing processes. Therefore, in addition to the usual measures of financial impact, the impact of lean on your company's operations must be evaluated from the individual function level all the way up through the system in order to maintain leanness in a constantly changing environment.

To be lean is to be "waste free" throughout your entire system. Every activity is purposefully and productively driven towards value for the customer. The system itself is dynamic and responsive, continually evaluating its processes and continuously reducing waste in its mission to provide value and quality to customers. In addition to the lean operations described above, a lean system must have three other key elements:

- Value
- Quality
- Process flow

Value

Value to wholesaler-distributors may not be the same as value recognized by customers. Value is exchanged when products or services offered meet customers' needs in return for their investment. What's more, traditional definitions of value must be viewed from the customer's perspective. To customers, a distributor's added value is realized when products or services are available when, where, and how they are needed. The distribution channel's value stream includes all of the steps necessary to meet customers' needs.

For example, a contractor in need of power tools calls his distributor to place an order. The distributor places the order for the tools and other supplies it stocks with a manufacturer that makes thousands of tools and accessories to sell around the world. The customer doesn't care how much it cost the manufacturer to make the tools or what logistical hoops the distributor jumped through to receive and distribute them. The contractor receives value when his tools fit his needs, both practically and financially.

Quality

In the customer's eyes, perceived quality equals value. Dr. John Nash explains perceived quality by saying, "The customer will judge value of a service (perceived quality) based on the utilities received in exchange for capital and effort" (Nash, 1996). In other words, the cost will be compared to the usefulness and suitability of the product or service the customer received, independent of the type of distribution. Essentially, perceived value is very often equated to the quality of the product or service received.

The quality of a wholesaler-distributor's products and services is recognized by providing what customers want, when and where customers want it, and how they want it—and these are the criteria on which a process model is evaluated.

David Garvin proposed eight dimensions of quality, later expanded to 14, to measure the quality of the products or services generated by a company's process model (Moen et. al., 1991):

1. Performance
2. Features
3. Time
4. Reliability
5. Durability
6. Uniformity
7. Consistency
8. Serviceability
9. Aesthetics
10. Personal interface
11. Harmlessness
12. Flexibility
13. Usability
14. Perceived quality.

From the distributor's perspective, each of these dimensions of quality translates to producing the what, when, where, and how of the customer's needs. In the pursuit of lean, your internal quality cannot be neglected. It too must be designed and measured in the context of the end user's perceived quality, as well as for the users within your company (in this case, your various departments and functions—your internal customers). The internal quality is the waste-free production of the services or products measured as a percentage of the available resources. This internal quality determines how well you use your resources to produce the final product or service and, in the process, turns the effort into capital and cash flow.

PROCESS FLOW

Interruptions to the smooth flow of material, information, and work through the system both add cost and reduce value. A distributor that is pursuing lean has a value flow with minimal interruptions.

Agile Distribution®

In a lean organization, which should be supported by excellent communication, the flow will follow an ideal path that is both predictable and repeatable, with strict adherence to procedure and process.

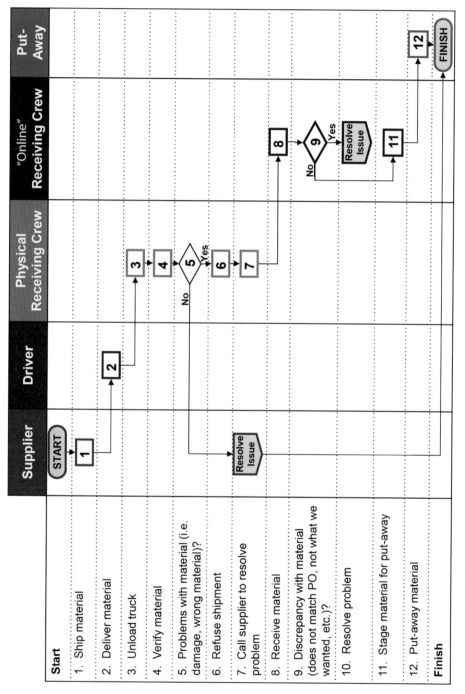

Exhibit 2-2. Deployment Flowchart.

27

For example, one distributor's receiving process is shown as a deployment flow chart in exhibit 2-2 (deployment flow charts will be described in detail in chapter 4). Across the top, the flow chart identifies the departments involved; the left most column identifies each of the steps or procedures that occur in the completion of the process. The ideal path starts at the top and smoothly flows to the bottom. One way to understand the flow is to evaluate a high-level view of the process:

- Can an uninterrupted line be drawn through the process?
- Does the flow of the process follow a logical sequence of events?
- Does the final product get to the customer without interruptions, waiting, rework, or revisions?
- By comparing the "ideal flow" to the reality of a current situation flow, a distributor can identify deviations and also where they occur. For example, does material or labor flow back and forth without acquiring additional value? Does one function dominate an entire process, or does the material transition smoothly through appropriate departments and functions within the departments?

In a lean distribution company culture, the flow of the system is measured by the capacity of the system as determined at the customer end—at the output—rather than at the input. The flow will support a functioning value-based "pull," where the requirements of each step of the process are determined by downstream demand: A customer's need for products or services triggers the delivery process, which triggers the order-production process, which triggers the order-entry process, which triggers the purchasing process, and so on back up the line.

This downstream demand structure is known as a "pull system" or "justified for the time of delivery" (Daneshgari, 1998). The needs and the capacity of each functional step are communicated to all other functions within the process so that the wholesaler-distributor can apply necessary resources to meet the customer's request in an efficient process with minimal waste. The distributor's system must be agile in order to facilitate the pull system, allowing each step in the process to quickly respond to increases or decreases in downstream demand.

In contrast, a method that produces without regard to downstream demand is known as a "push system." Where a push process forces the distributor's resources to react to, for example, a forecast based on past performance, a pull process relies on customer input and buying habits to determine operational needs. Exhibits 2-3 and 2-4 illustrate the differences between a push delivery system and a pull delivery system.

The differences between the two systems can be seen in the transition from purchasing to the warehouse:

Push (inventory build-up in the warehouse):

- Purchasing places an order for material
- Material arrives
- Material is received into inventory
- Accounts payable receives an invoice
- A customer may (or may not) arrive to purchase the material.

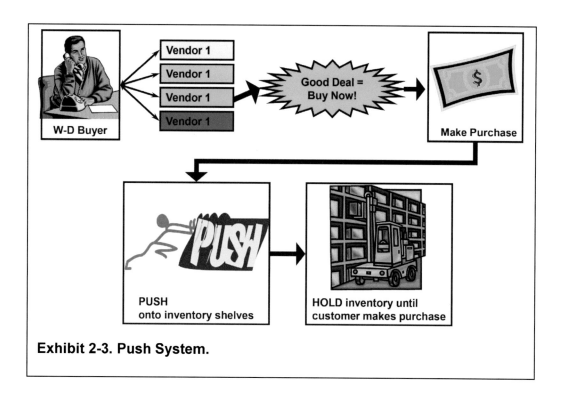

Exhibit 2-3. Push System.

Pull (cell design):

- Customer buying habits are known
- Customer arrives to purchase material
- Material is pulled from inventory
- Inventory change signals a need to replace buffer
- Purchasing places orders to replace buffer
- Needed material arrives.

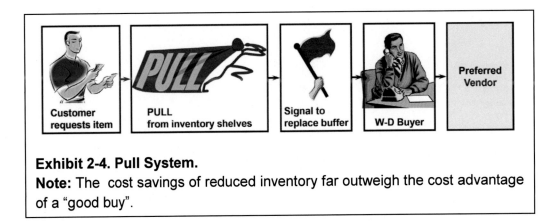

Exhibit 2-4. Pull System.
Note: The cost savings of reduced inventory far outweigh the cost advantage of a "good buy".

In a lean culture, the system fully supports the pull of customer value through your entire system, while reducing or eliminating waste. In the pull example above, inventory flowing through your system is now determined by customers' needs rather than purchasing availability. This revised, streamlined approach to managing inventory is just one example of the importance of lean operations to wholesaler-distributors.

The next chapter describes why distributors should pursue lean and describes some of the measurements and tools distributors can use to implement the process.

CHAPTER 3

Why Should You Pursue Lean?

In its simplest form, a lean process can be described as doing the right things (no waste) in the right way (no errors), so the opportunities come in two primary forms:

- Reducing and eliminating waste
- Reducing and eliminating errors

These two objectives clear the way to adding value, which is your primary goal as a wholesaler-distributor. This is why it's essential for you to implement a lean culture and pursue lean operations.

Each step in the wholesale distribution order processing system consists of individual procedures, each of which must be designed to support lean concepts and flow. Your many processes, procedures, and tasks must be smoothly integrated, with the common priority of creating the flow that provides value to customers. This requires ongoing monitoring and measuring of your systems, with the ultimate goal of continuous improvement. Essentially, you must identify opportunities for becoming leaner within each department and then apply the tools and methods that can help you achieve your goals.

This chapter describes some of the key measurements and tools distributors can use to pursue lean. But first, it's important to lay the groundwork by describing the nature and impact of waste and errors in wholesale distribution.

Waste

Waste can be manifested physically, in terms of material or money, or less tangibly, in terms of effort, such as wasted labor or poorly allocated equipment time.

Waste is a natural and normal byproduct of distributor operations that exists as a result of any of the following circumstances:

- Rework:
    1. Repeating any activity or step of a process
    2. Picking, re-shelving, then re-picking
    3. Defects/rejects
    4. Items or activities that are completed incorrectly
    5. Double shipping, handling damage, delivery of incorrect materials
- Over Capacity:
    1. More capacity than needed to meet the needs of the customer or market
    2. Too much space, too many people, too many trucks
- Transportation:
    1. Movement of material that does not add value
    2. Carrying material up and down aisles or from far corners.
- Motion:
    1. Physical movement of the person that does not add value
    2. Climbing, reaching, bending, stretching.
- Waiting:
    1. Idle time created when material, information, or people are not ready or available
    2. Waiting for tickets to drop.
- Excess Inventory:
    1. Excess anywhere in the cycle: in stock, on order, in transit, in process
    2. Zone warehousing.
- Overprocessing (Overengineering):
    1. Effort that creates no value from the customer's point of view
    2. Overpackaging.

All of your activities can be classified in one of three categories:

- Value-added (to the customer)
- Non-value-added but necessary (due to regulations or other requirements)
- Non-value-added and not necessary

Value-added activities are those that the customer recognizes as adding value—activities that move the product closer to the customer in terms of the what, when, how. and where he needs it: picking, packaging, loading.

Non-value-added but necessary activities are those that do not add specific value for customers, yet the system cannot function without them. Poor design often adds unnecessary work that masquerades as a requirement. For example, customers don't receive additional value from a worker walking to the far corner of the warehouse to retrieve material, yet the layout may dictate that the material cannot be picked without the worker doing exactly that. Non-value-added and non-necessary activities include rework, error correction, and other forms of waste in terms of manpower, money, or materials.

Non-value-added work from the customer's perspective includes:

- Calling the salesperson to confirm an address
- Walking to the second floor to locate the necessary material.

Non-value-added work that may be required by the system and current processes may include:

- Documenting an order on a delivery log
- Scanning material into an inventory system
- Labeling an outgoing package with the specifics of delivery
- Loading trucks.

Value-added activities are only those that move the product closer to the customer, for example:

- Picking correct material from the shelf
- Packaging or staging to meet customers' needs
- Delivering material.

From an organizational perspective, financial waste is often one of the least visible, but most costly, forms of waste. Persistent claims, slow collections, and excessive product inventories all represent common and costly misuse of your financial resources. Other important, less visible sources of resource waste include:

- The expensive resource cost of a salesperson making an emergency delivery
- The non-value-added time warehouse personnel spend searching for material
- The rework associated with errors entering the system anywhere from order entry to final collection on the bill.

Errors

Errors are exactly that—mistakes; something done incorrectly:

- A correct delivery to the correct customer, minus one item left on the truck
- An order pulled for the wrong color item
- An order entered with the wrong quantity
- A delivery made to the wrong location.

Errors are costly, as the full effort of processing a correct order has been devoted to an order that will have to be redone. Errors recognized at the end of the process are the most costly—the cost is more than three times the cost of processing correctly the first time through because you go through the following steps:

- You use the resources needed to process the original order incorrectly
- You use the same resources (or more, as corrections often occur outside the system) to re-process correctly
- You lose key opportunities by applying those resources to rework instead of new value-added activities.

In looking at waste and errors, measurement becomes a key tool in pursuing lean.

System Measurements

Quality is nothing less than: "Translating needs of the customer into measurable characteristics" (Moen, Nolan and Provost, 1991, 3). By the same token, distributors must measure the "quality of leanness" in their organizations. Key measurement terms include:

- First-Time Pass
- Capacity, Capability, and Throughput
- Cycle Time
- Takt Time.

All of these terms are explained in this chapter and defined in the glossary.

First-Time Pass

First-time pass, also called system yield, measures the errors that occur at each step in a process or procedure. A lean process occurs when first-time pass yield is nearing 100%: Rework and non-essential steps have been eliminated and capacity is efficiently utilized. This measurement is a critical indicator of how well you utilize your resources to deliver the final product or service.

First-time pass must be measured backward from the end of the process: How many orders went entirely through the system with no rework or errors at any stage. Both "correct but incomplete" orders and "incorrect" orders begin to generate additional work and additional cost, even if they are immediately caught and corrected. The time spent processing an incomplete or incorrect order can never be recovered.

Suppose the steps of the distribution process are as simple as:

1. Enter order (in sales).
2. Process order (in warehouse).
3. Deliver order (to customer).

Exhibit 3-1 shows this three-step order-production process as simplified to sales, warehouse, and delivery and its possible rework loops. In this process, only those items that went through the entire system completely and correctly are measured when calculating first-time pass yield. The items that do not make it through the system correctly in the first time pass fall into various error categories in terms of when they occur and when they are recognized.

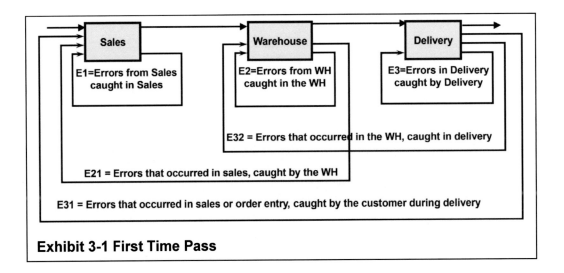

Exhibit 3-1 First Time Pass

Exhibit 3-1 works as follows: Errors may occur that are immediately caught and corrected at any stage of the process—for example, pulling a wrong item from a shelf and immediately putting it back and pulling the correct item from an adjacent shelf. Another example is leaving an item on the truck during delivery, but recognizing and correcting the issue before the truck leaves the delivery location. These single-step errors often are not even captured or identified, because typical measurements capture errors only between steps. In exhibit 3-1, these single-step errors are shown as follows:

- **E1:** Items with errors that were created during sales and were caught and corrected during the sales process
- **E2:** Items with errors that were created in the warehouse process and were caught and corrected during the warehouse process
- **E3:** Items with errors that were created during delivery and were caught and corrected during the delivery process.

Other errors that occur at one stage may be caught in the next and sent back for correction. For example, an item incorrectly entered in a quantity of 10 that is typically sold in quantities of 1,000 may be caught as an error in the warehouse; or, a correct delivery could be attempted with an incorrect item. Exhibit 3-1 shows examples of these rework loops as:

- **E21:** Items with errors that were created in the sales area and were caught and corrected in the warehouse area;
- **E32:** Items with errors that were created in the warehouse area and were caught and corrected in the delivery area.

If the entry error is not caught—either as it is being entered or in the warehouse as it is being pulled—it could also be correctly processed as a ticket for 10 of the items and not caught until it is delivered and the customer asks for the other 990. This is shown in exhibit 3-1 as the rework loop from delivery all the way back to sales:

- **E31:** Items with errors that were created in the sales area and were caught and corrected in the delivery area.

Items carrying errors through the system require a complete second cycle to correct the issue—a new order must be entered, the items repulled in the warehouse, and another delivery made to provide the customer with the full 1,000 items ordered. In addition, the distributor must absorb the cost and effort allocated to identifying the source of the miscommunication. The original second step is waste. Although it was correctly processed, it was the correct processing of an incorrect order. The time spent correctly processing the order for 10 is not recoverable.

The first-time pass yield for this simplified system would be calculated as follows:

- All orders into the system
- Less the number of orders with errors caught and corrected in the same step (E1, E2, E3)
- Less the number of orders with errors caught in the step immediately after its occurrence (E21, E32)
- Less the number of orders with errors caught two steps after its occurrence (E31).

Exhibit 3-1 shows how quickly these compounding errors convolute the system, adding cost and complexity at every step. See appendix B for a more detailed explanation and calculation of first-time pass yield.

Capacity, Capability, and Throughput

The capacity of your system is measured by the maximum production (the number of orders, lines, deliveries, and so on) that can be processed through the system at peak efficiency. The capability measures how many orders can be processed with current operational practices and efficiencies. And throughput is measured by how much input material has been converted into sales.

Together, waste and errors greatly reduce the capability of your system by restricting throughput. All activities that divert resources into non-value-added activities impair your company's productivity. This will always result in increased waste, thereby reducing the output compared to the resources.

By reducing waste and improving the first-time pass yield, the capability of the system can be increased, allowing you to process more: More deliveries, more lines, and more orders—more efficiently using the same resources.

What's more, profitability in a fixed-cost model, such as that in wholesale distribution, is determined by the capability and throughput of the system. How the resources are used becomes more important than how many resources there are.

For example, suppose a company needs to process 100 orders. If at the end of the day, the company produces the full 100 orders—no matter how much effort was involved—the system must have had the capability to produce all 100 orders. In a perfect system, this can be done if the capacity supports only the 100 orders. In reality, the situation is much different. The capacity of the system must be large enough to not only produce the 100 orders correctly, but also to expend the non-value-added effort required to correct a sufficient number of orders to compensate for all errors introduced at any point in the system.

Assuming that 60% of your company's effort is value-added and 95% of your output is correct (first-time pass), the impact of waste and rework on your system's capability is shown in exhibit 3-2. (As with exhibit 2-1, this exhibit must be read from right to left, indicating the distributor's response to customer input.)Your system would need to possess the capacity for processing 175 orders in order to actually produce the required 100 orders.

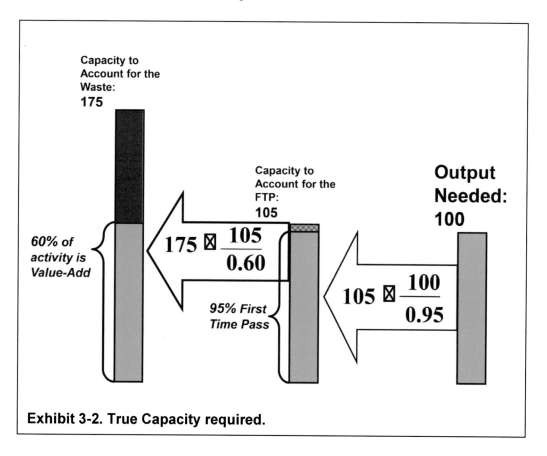

Exhibit 3-2. True Capacity required.

In reality, this scenario translates into much higher numbers. For example, a study at one distributor recognized that, on average, 1.5% of its picking attempts failed to show the correct location of material that was listed as "available" in the inventory system. Its system automatically issued back orders to reacquire the material, even if the material was available elsewhere in the warehouse. Processing the back order sent that line item back through the entire system as a new order. In addition, 71% of the effort expended by pullers in an average ticket pull was found to be non-value-added time (either wholly unproductive or unproductive from the customer's point of view, yet required by the warehouse system in place). If this warehouse was required to produce 1,000 lines on a typical day, 1,015 needed to be processed in order to end up with the 1,000. However, since 71% of the pulling effort was non-value-added, the system actually had the capacity to pull a full 3,500 lines with the same resources (exhibit 3-3).

$$\frac{1{,}015 \text{ (lines picked per day to get 1,000 correct lines)}}{29\% \text{ (portion of picking effort that is Non-Value-Add activity)}} = 3{,}500$$

lines per day
= true capacity of warehouse with 100% FTP and 100% Value-Add effort

Exhibit 3-3 First Time Pass and waste compounded.

Once the problem was evident, this distributor was able to make important changes to its picking system. The company revised its receiving and put-away processes, drastically reducing the number of "pick exceptions," eliminating some of the system rework, and increasing the capability by freeing the resources to complete tickets. In addition, the distributor redesigned its system to reduce some of the primary components of the 71% wasted effort. Between the two initiatives, the distributor increased its productivity and significantly increased the capability and throughput of its warehouse by doing no more than utilizing the capacity it already had.

But the ticket-pulling component is only one step of the warehouse process, which is only one step of the distribution system. Recall the previous example of a three-step process (outlined in the first-time pass example in exhibit 3-1). If each step has the same limitations, the impact multiplies. If each stage of the operation—sales, order entry, and delivery—operates about 95% correctly, the entire system only operates at 95% times 95% times 95%, or only about 85% correctly, as a result of the waste and rework. The rework loops of exhibit 3-1 show that some of the correct effort in the warehouse and delivery stages may actually be applied to orders that were incorrectly entered. What's more, orders that were correctly entered may have had to be reentered to correct an error that came in at a later stage.

In reality, the distribution process is far more involved than three steps. The bottom line is that errors and waste at each step of the system get compounded as you go along, adding cost for the distributor and reducing value for the customer. For example, at 10 steps, if each step operates at 95% correct, the entire process yield (or first-time pass) will drop to less than 60%—before taking into account the added capacity from solely value-added effort. In other words, of every 100 orders or lines correctly sent through the system, 40 have had an error introduced then corrected between transition points. Exhibit 3-4 shows the end result of the compounded errors in this process.

Exhibit 3-4. System First-time pass (FTP).

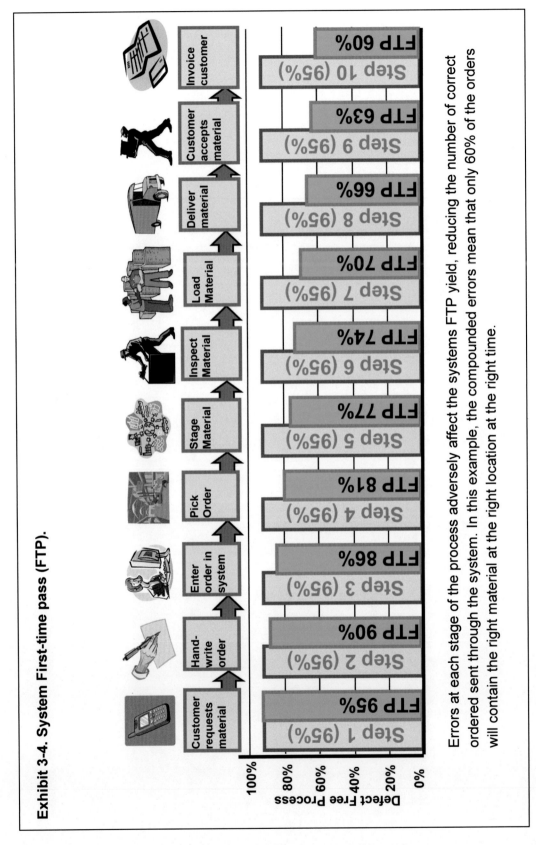

Errors at each stage of the process adversely affect the systems FTP yield, reducing the number of correct ordered sent through the system. In this example, the compounded errors mean that only 60% of the orders will contain the right material at the right location at the right time.

Cycle Time

Little's Law of Response. System cycle time is another important tool. One measure of system cycle time calculates the processing time of orders in the distribution system based on the queuing principle. (The processing time refers to the time it takes from order entry through delivery, encompassing everything from picking the order, to fabrication work—for distributors in certain lines of trade—to packaging the order and preparing it for shipment.) This principle, also known as Little's Law of Response, is one of the governing laws of system design.

Little's Law states: The average number of orders in a queuing system—the "work in process" (WIP)—is equal to the average "output rate" (OR) of orders from that system times the average time spent in that system—the "system cycle time" (SCT). The work in process has been sold, but at this point the material is being carried by the company as hidden inventory: The material is no longer available for sales (no longer an asset) and is not yet recognized as revenue. When distributors reduce the work in process by compacting the cycle time, hidden inventory is more quickly converted into sales. The Little's Law equation looks like this: **SCT = WIP x OR**.

For example, one distributor processes on average of 200 orders—or roughly 2,400 line items (an average of 12 lines per order)—per 8-hour shift. An average line item generates $170 in revenue. Each order takes an average of 20 minutes to process from order entry through pickup. The 200 orders times 20 minutes (or .33 hours) equates to a WIP of 66.67 orders. At $170 per line times 12 lines per order, the dollar value for the WIP is $136,068 at any given time. Again, this money is tied up in inventory. Since only 60% of the cycle time is actually value-added to the customer, applying lean concepts that will reduce the cycle time for each order to 12 minutes will also reduce the WIP by 40%—to $81,640 in tied-up inventory. The difference of $54,427 is returned to usable capital assets. Exhibit 3-5 illustrates this example.

Exhibit 3-5. Little's Law/WIP calculation.

Distributor's Fixed Values:

Output Rate (OR) = 200 orders processed per 8-hour shift
= 2,400 lines (average 12 lines per order)

Average Revenue = $170 per line

System Cycle Time (SCT) = 20 minutes (from order entry to pickup) or .33 hours

Step 1: Calculate work in process (WIP):
SCT (.33) x OR (200) = WIP (66 orders)

Step 2: Calculate total number of lines:
66 orders x 12 lines per order = 792 lines

Step 3: Calculate WIP dollar value:
792 lines x $170 per line = $134,640

If SCT is reduced to 12 minutes per order (or .2 hours per order):

Step 1: Calculate WIP:
SCT (.2) x OR (200) = 40 orders

Step 2: Calculate total lines:
40 orders x 12 lines per order = 480 lines

Step 3: Calculate WIP dollar value:
480 x $170 per line = $81,600

Step 4: Calculate WIP reduction, in dollars:
$134,640 – $81,600 = $53,040

Queuing orders in your system is expensive. If this system is fast enough so that the output rate is equal to the system throughput, requests will not be queued and hidden inventory will be minimized. At the point where the throughput is equal to or higher than the output rate, 100% utilization of the system has been achieved.

You must evaluate your system in order to implement a lean process flow throughout your company. You can do this by applying Little's Law, which is the underlying principle in designing such a process flow in any organization. To do this, you must first test your systems.

When load-testing, or stress-testing, a system, the only variable that can be controlled is the output rate. Variables that must be measured include throughput, response time, and the number of completed requests in a period of time. The application of Little's Law in a warehouse environment is shown in the following example:

Suppose an order is placed for material that will be arriving into the warehouse today. For the puller to pull this material, it must first be received into the system. The amount of time it will take to receive this material is almost entirely based upon the backlog of incoming shipments for that day at the warehouse. Exhibits 3-6 and 3-7 below demonstrate this process.

For example, if it takes 1 minute to unload and verify a pallet of inbound freight, 1 minute to stage the pallet of material in an aisle to be put away, and 1 more minute to put the pallet away on the shelves, then that means it will take a total of 3 minutes to complete the receiving and stocking of that particular shipment (exhibit 3-6).

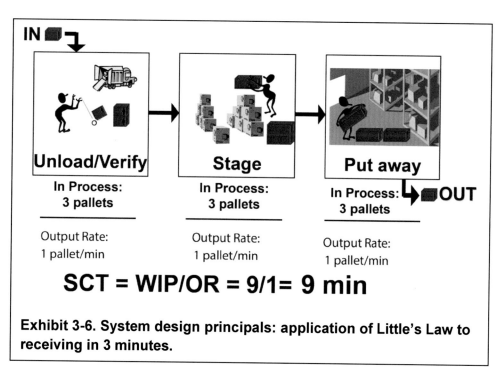

Exhibit 3-6. System design principals: application of Little's Law to receiving in 3 minutes.

However, if there are three pallets already waiting to be offloaded, three other pallets waiting to be staged, and still three more pallets waiting to be put away, the total time it will take to receive the shipment is now 9 minutes (exhibit 3-7).

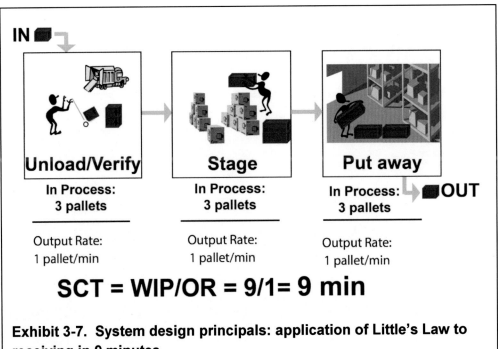

IN

Unload/Verify	Stage	Put away
In Process:	**In Process:**	**In Process:** **OUT**
3 pallets	**3 pallets**	**3 pallets**
Output Rate:	Output Rate:	Output Rate:
1 pallet/min	1 pallet/min	1 pallet/min

$$SCT = WIP/OR = 9/1 = 9 \text{ min}$$

Exhibit 3-7. System design principals: application of Little's Law to receiving in 9 minutes.

When you increase the amount of work at each phase of the process, you increase the amount of time it takes to complete each incoming task. In this case, the system cycle time increases from 3 minutes to 9 minutes simply because there is additional work in the system. The bottom line is that too much work in front of one worker means that any new work added to the queue will take longer. Recognizing that this is only for the receiving procedure, similar backups cause delays at every step in warehouse production.

As another example, consider the administrative workflow in sales, purchasing, or accounting. If each associate in exhibit 3-8 can process one document per minute and has four items backlogged, then any new document added to that associate's workload will now take a total of 16 minutes to go through the cycle. This is because each new document must start at the bottom of the pile and wait its turn to go through the system.

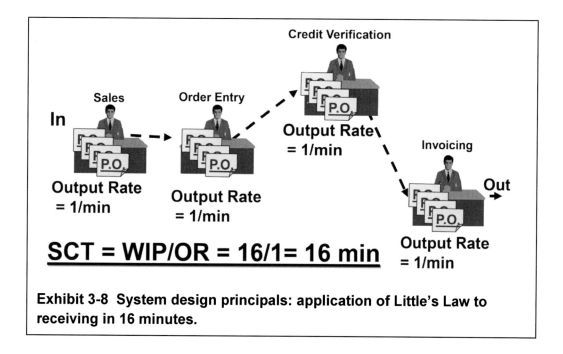

Exhibit 3-8 System design principals: application of Little's Law to receiving in 16 minutes.

If the process is set up so that each associate works on one item at a time, any new item will only require 4 minutes to get through the system. This allows for a 75% improvement of workflow without an increase in workload. Once the system is designed with the flow of products and services in mind, the throughput will increase automatically. Tickets are pulled more efficiently, bills are sent out more

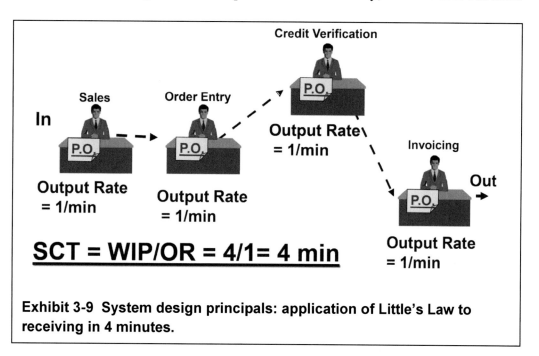

Exhibit 3-9 System design principals: application of Little's Law to receiving in 4 minutes.

efficiently, and orders are entered more efficiently. Exhibit 3-9 illustrates the smoother, more efficient process.

Takt Time

Takt time, derived from the German word *taktzeit*, or "beat time," measures a different cycle. Takt time is the maximum time allowed to produce an order to meet demand. In a lean distributorship, the pace of the order flow will be determined to best respond to this takt time or demand cycle time. The product flow cycle should be no longer than the takt time.

Takt time is a theoretical calculation determined by dividing the available production time by the rate of customer demand (output demand). The most practical method for determining takt time is to simply observe the system in operation to measure the time required for each step and each activity. For example, if customers purchase 2,000 different line items per day and your warehouse operates with 10 employees for two 8-hour shifts every day (a total of 160 hours, or 9,600 minutes of production time), your takt time is 4.8 minutes (exhibit 3-10). In other words, individual items must be received, stocked, pulled, and loaded for delivery every 4.8 minutes. The calculation of takt time should only use available production time, subtracting time spent on breaks, lunch, and so forth.

Takt Time for Production	
Customer Demand for Items =	2,000 lines / day
Available Time for Production = 8 Hours Per Shift X 2 Shifts Per Day X 10 Workers Per Shift	160 hours = 9,600 minutes
Takt Time = Available Working Time / Customer Demand	4.8 minutes

Exhibit 3-10. Takt time calculation example.

If your warehouse performs this production sequence more than once every 4.8 minutes, it is overproducing, which could lead to unnecessary inventory. If it operates at a slower pace, the warehouse is under producing, which could lead to back orders or stock outs when the order is not completed according to demand. Both cases result in waste: excess inventory, unnecessary production, rework, and extra steps. Waste in the system requires additional resources to satisfy customer demand and results in increased cost.

Takt time has direct implications on the allowable time for completing individual steps in the order process. This is the case for both steps that modify (form, assemble, finish) the product and those that observe and control (test, measure, adjust) the process. For example, steps that require assembly, or a part of the product to have been put into an accurately fixed position, must be completed in less than the total takt time—this is so that time is allowed to load and unload, or position, the part in addition to the time for actually performing the step. The quicker a measurement or test step can be completed, the less constraint is placed upon motion between steps.

Distributors must test their systems and measure those systems' capabilities in order to implement lean. And it doesn't end there. Testing and measuring are ongoing components of a lean system. The section below discusses companywide operational measurements that help wholesaler-distributors become leaner, with particular emphasis on customers.

Operational Measurements

Once a company initiates a lean strategy, the ongoing challenge is to stay lean as customer needs evolve. Companywide operational measurements become an increasingly important addition to the financial picture. These measurements must go beyond those typically used by wholesaler-distributors. For example, using only financial measurements, such as Weighted Average Cost of Capital, does not give an operational overview, and traditional measures such as Activity Based Costing, in addition to being cumbersome and inaccurate, often focus only on variable costs.

Since the wholesaler-distributor's cost structure is primarily a fixed-cost model, operational measurements need to recognize resource utilization: How effectively do you apply your resources? One way to determine this is by using Customer Positioning and Control (CPAC®), a reliable method for measuring the requirements, in terms of both cost and effort, necessary to meet customer demands--whether that customer is external (an end customer) or internal (another department or supply chain element). In addition, CPAC® measures the impact of these customer demands on the company's overall operational profitability.

Branches, divisions, projects, or customers can be easily compared using CPAC®. Areas of strength and weakness become clearly visible. Services can be priced according to costs. As plans are implemented to address areas of insufficient profits or significant costs, CPAC® provides a method for monitoring the effects of those changes over time.

Customer Positioning and Control

The following section describes CPAC® and what it can do for distributors.

CPAC® requires you to chart what you are analyzing on a four-quadrant graph. You could decide to measure customer performance, for example—how well your top customers perform in terms of the resources you devote to those customers. Dr. John Nash's "Game Theory" was used to develop the four quadrants of the system (Nash, 1996). Game Theory describes the customer's perspective on the products and services he receives: "The customer will judge value of a service (perceived quality) based on the utilities received in exchange for capital and effort." The reverse is also true; a distributor's profitable customers are those that use the least amount of capital and effort (resources) for the services or products provided.

In other words, happy customers are profitable customers, and unhappy customers are usually very costly customers. CPAC® can show you how this plays out among your customer base.

CPAC®'s four-quadrant positioning method evaluates customers or operations based on profits and revenues. This discussion will focus on customers. For example, the components involved in serving a particular customer are divided into cost codes according to the type of work required—your sales, warehouse, delivery, and administration departments are cost codes tied to each customer. Based on internal data, you then determine how much that customer "costs" you in terms of labor and dollars for each of those functions.

Once these measurements are determined, you can chart the customers in the four quadrants of the graph. The graph must include a reference point to benchmark performance. Reference points can be budget goals, break-even points, or industry wide performance averages, for instance.

Exhibit 3-11 shows what a finished four-quadrant model looks like for one distributor. Customers in quadrant 1 generate high revenue per hour spent servicing them and per cost to serve them. Essentially, servicing this customer is a lean operation: The distributor generates very few errors in delivering products and services to this customer (that is, first-time pass is good); there is very little waste involved in servicing this customer; and the distributor anticipates the customer's needs well.

Customers in quadrant 2 generate high revenue per cost, but low revenue per hour spent serving the customer. Essentially, there is a lot of wasted effort involved in servicing this customer. The distributor needs to eliminate some of that waste.

Customers in quadrant 3 generate high revenue per hour but low revenue per cost. Essentially, there is a lot of rework involved in servicing this customer.

Customers in quadrant 4 generate low revenue per hour and per cost. Servicing these customers requires significant rework and involves significant waste.

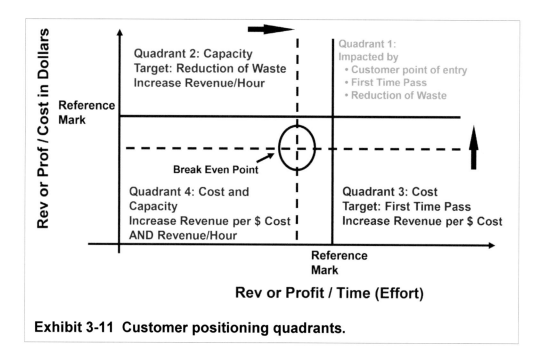

Exhibit 3-11 Customer positioning quadrants.

Looked at another way, exhibit 3-12 shows three customers positioned against a target revenue goal; this shows how much revenue each customer is generating according to the resources they use. While customer 3 (C3) is doing well in terms of revenue generation, customers 1 (C1) and 2 (C2) are below revenue targets, which is not necessarily the most effective use of resource time.

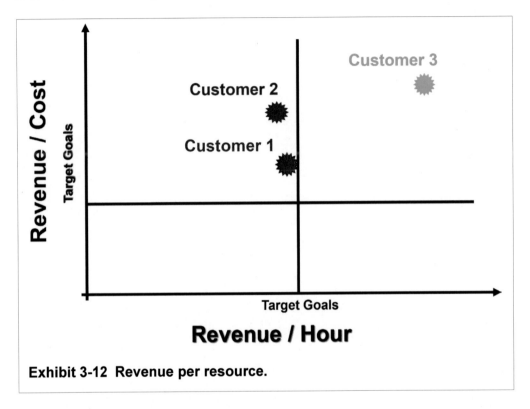

Exhibit 3-12 Revenue per resource.

CPAC® can also identify customers providing sufficient revenue but insufficient profits. In exhibit 3-12, all three customers were better than fourth quadrant, but only C3 was well positioned above the target revenue goals. If the distributor reevaluates the customers based on profits instead of revenues, C3 could well end up in quadrant 4, meaning that while it generates a lot of revenue, the customer is a drag on the distributor's financial resources and time. Exhibit 3-13 shows what this evaluation would look like.

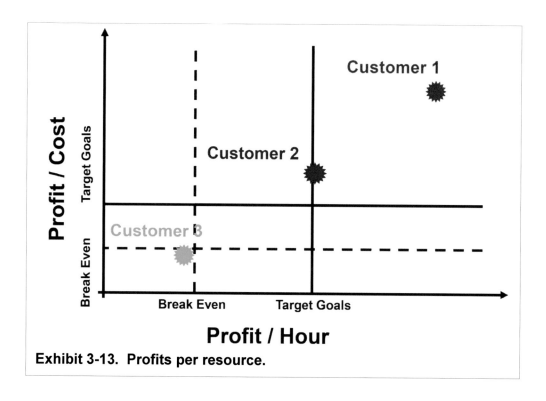

Exhibit 3-13. Profits per resource.

Each customer can be further analyzed to see which of the distributor's departments or functions—sales, warehouse, delivery and administration, as noted previously—are the highest cost drivers for that account. Again, using internal data, the distributor can determine how much time per hour and per cost each department spends servicing that customer. Those departments are then charted in the four quadrants, as shown in exhibit 3-14. In this example, the sales and administration departments are performing well, but improvements can be made in delivery and in the warehouse.

The periodic positioning of customers and their cost drivers over time will identify and measure changes in order to evaluate improvements. Each customer can be tracked at a cost-code level, repositioning on a periodic basis (weekly, monthly, or at defined intervals) to identify and measure progress or declines in each of the areas and overall.

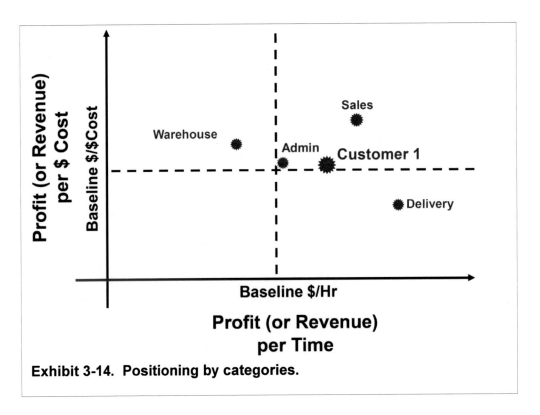

Exhibit 3-14. Positioning by categories.

CPAC®'s flexibility also allows a number of other applications that follow the basic CPAC® guidelines of positioning and trend monitoring. Distributors can do the following:

- Make relative comparisons
    1. What factors make one customer better than another?
    2. How are resources utilized on one customer compared to another?
    3. How do customers compare with respect to realized profits or revenues as a return for effort and cost?
- Compare a project or customer to a template
    1. What configuration makes a good customer?
- Grouping of work
    1. Which customers, types of work, size of projects, and so on, realize insufficient profits or revenues as a return for effort and cost?
- Resource evaluation
    1. Where might additional resources need to be deployed?
    2. Which resources are being used to capacity?
    3. Which resources are being underutilized?

The CPAC® model is a vital tool in monitoring your journey toward lean operations.

The next chapter discusses how to apply lean principles in a distribution environment and is followed by examples of how national, regional and local distributors have used lean principles to improve operations.

CHAPTER 4

How to Apply Lean

Lean operations are not niceties; they are necessities for a profitable distributorship. Understanding the requirement for correct, relevant measurements is only the first step in applying lean. The next step is applying tools and methods to facilitate the development of lean operations. This chapter describes the lean implementation process and is followed by some real-world examples in chapters 5, 6, and 7.

STRATEGIC BREAKTHROUGH PROCESS IMPROVEMENT

As distributors, you cannot stop your operations to apply lean concepts. The Strategic Breakthrough Process Improvement (SBPI®) method allows you to apply the principles of lean operations in manageable sections—without losing sight of the overall transformation.

Essentially, by systematically applying the phases and deliverables of the SBPI® process, distributors can transform themselves into near-perfect delivery systems for products and services.

The four phases of SBPI® implementation are

1. Identification
2. Characterization
3. Optimization
4. Utilization.

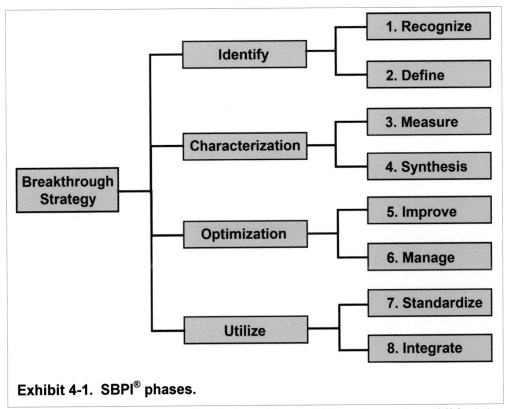

Exhibit 4-1. SBPI® phases.

Each phase supports two major deliverable activities, shown in exhibit 4-1 and discussed below.

Together these activities provide a structure for first identifying areas with opportunities for improvement within your company, and then defining the scope, impact, and outcome of any lean project you undertake. Individual lean projects are often referred to as "kaizen events." *Kaizen* is a Japanese term that in English is most often translated as "continuous improvement." A kaizen event aims to improve a process, procedure, or particular job function. (See the glossary for more information about kaizen.)Learning tools (such as Plan-Do-Study-Act cycles, described below) and operational measurement and process control tools (such as CPAC®, described in chapter 3) are used during these events and they allow you to do two key things:

- Build a learning organization that fosters continuous study and improvement through designed processes and control points.
- Ultimately utilize standardized processes and improvement strategies throughout your organization.

Exhibit 4-2 describes the steps involved in the SBPI® process.

Exhibit 4-2. Strategic Breakthrough Process Improvement.

	Identify		Characterize		Optimize		Utilize	
Initiative Start-up	Recognize	Define	Measure	Synthesize	Improve	Manage	Standardize	Integrate
Step 0	**Step 1**	**Step 2**	**Step 3**	**Step 4**	**Step 5**	**Step 6**	**Step 7**	**Step 8**
• Steering committee • Implementation team — Production — Inventory — Inspection • Select team members • Bring team together • Brainstorm issues	• Process maps • Prioritized list of issues • Select top issues • Plan for gathering data on selected issues	• Overall opportunity selection • PDSA selection • Plan tests	• Measurement methods • Perform tests • Collect data • Issue resolution process	• Study/Analyze data • PDSA reports • Accept/Reject • Concept selection • Pilot selection	• Review success of pilot • Authorization to proceed • Expanded pilots as required	• ERP/Dashboard • Quality circles • Project plans	• Test across organization • Risks identified • Risk management plan • Replication plans	• Fully incorporate into regular operations

Identify: Recognize and Define

Recognizing performance shortcomings from the customer's perspective is the first step to applying lean. The identification stage of the SBPI® process focuses on diagnosing the issues affecting the productivity and throughput of your system. This is done by recognizing the situation and defining the scope of the problem:

- What are the issues?
- What are the opportunities?
- How are they manifested?
- Which areas are involved?
- How extensively?

True issues and waste within the company are often hidden; that which appears to be the issue is frequently no more than an effect from a different problem entirely. For this reason, a clear definition of the problem is essential. For example, an incorrect delivery does not necessarily begin with the driver; it could come from incorrect material, incorrect loading, incorrect addresses, incorrect orders, and so on. Developing a cross-functional team of employees that can establish a broad view of the causes will help you identify major issues.

In addition, many issues affect multiple areas of the organization in a variety of ways. For example, the issue that may be the hottest topic for the shipping department may barely show up on the radar screen in sales or accounting. Prioritizing these issues must be done systematically to identify those areas that are not in line with your overall vision and mission. Without exception, this process must recognize each issue's impact on the customer. The prioritization needs to recognize each issue's potential impact on your profitability, productivity, and resource availability as well.

A "Fishbone Diagram"—or Ishikawa Diagram (Moen et al, 1991)— is one tool that can be used to analyze the root cause of a problem. Let's use back orders as an example—you want to figure out the root causes of back orders in your system. To create a fishbone diagram for this problem, you first gather a cross-functional team of employees from sales, warehouse, order processing, purchasing, accounting, credit, delivery, and any other department that is affected by the topic. The team will brainstorm and answer the question, "Why do backorders exist?" Members of the team should use sticky notes to write down any ideas that they may have (exhibit 4-3).

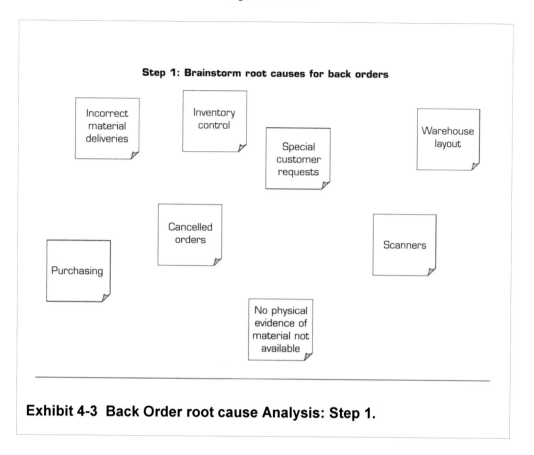

Exhibit 4-3 Back Order root cause Analysis: Step 1.

Next, the ideas should be grouped into the following categories—or root causes (exhibit 4-4):

- People
- Process
- Material
- Environment
- Tools.

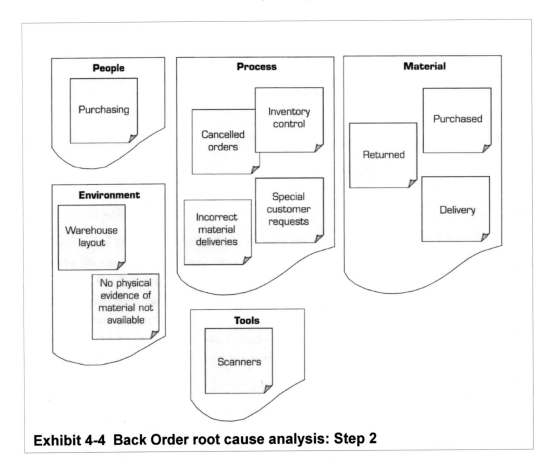

Exhibit 4-4 Back Order root cause analysis: Step 2

Next, you draw your fishbone diagram. A horizontal arrow points to the effect (in this case, back orders), and arrows representing the five root causes make up the "legs" of the diagram. The ideas your team identified in exhibit 4-4 should be written along the corresponding arrow on the diagram (exhibit 4-5).

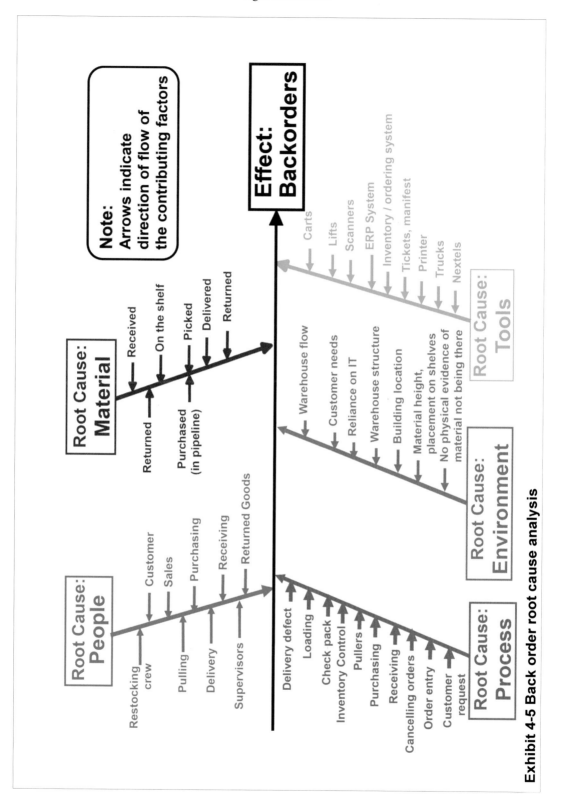

Exhibit 4-5 Back order root cause analysis

This diagram allows you to see what is causing back orders system wide. Understanding the most significant cause (in a broad sense) allows you to direct energy and effort to the underlying cause of the problem—whether it be process, personnel, tools, material, or the physical setting. In this case, "process" is the most significant issue affecting the back order problem, because it is the root cause with the most contributing factors.

To recognize the true roots of the issues, the process must be made visible with all connections and interactions clearly understood. The best approach to showing the connections is to develop a spaghetti chart that clearly identifies every function involved in a particular process and the communication network between and among them. Among the concerns the spaghetti chart will highlight are

- Multiple functions repeating the same activity
- Back and forth interaction between two areas
- One-way communication channels (dead ends)
- Significant communication needing to be routed through one functional position.

To create a spaghetti chart, your cross-functional team should identify all the functions/departments necessary to accomplish the activity you are analyzing (in this case, back orders, as show in exhibit 4-6).

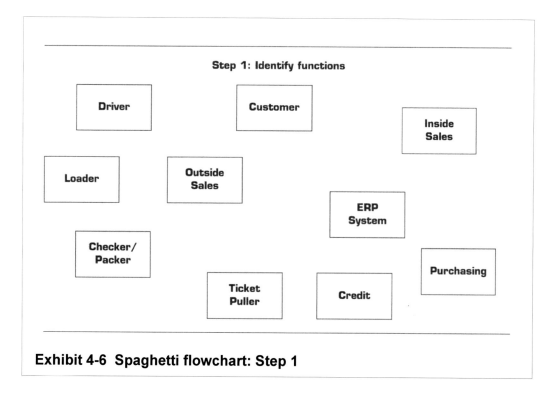

Exhibit 4-6 Spaghetti flowchart: Step 1

Once all the functions/departments are identified, the team should identify the lines of communication between those functions/departments (this is step 2). Essentially, the team is identifying the communication that takes place between these departments as it relates to back orders. In this case, the team might point to the following:

- Clarify questions on delivery
- Send quotes to customers
- Receive orders from customers
- Notification of pulling errors
- Check on inventory availability
- Submit orders
- Confirm orders
- Send credit verification.

Next, the lines of communication are connected to each function to show the flow of the information/documents between departments (exhibit 4-7). The department or function that has the highest number of lines coming or going out of it is probably the function/department that is the bottleneck and needs to be looked at for improvement.

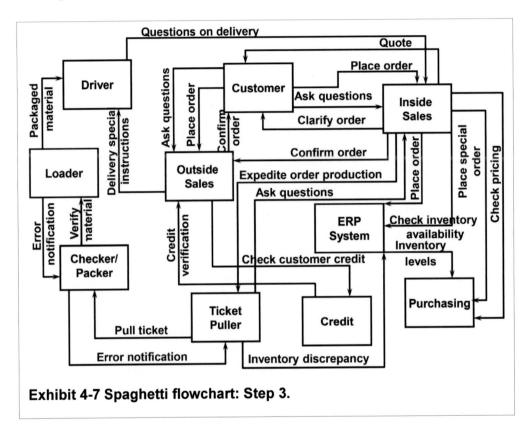

Exhibit 4-7 Spaghetti flowchart: Step 3.

From there, a deployment flowchart mapping the current process can help identify bottlenecks, convolutions in the process, excessive departures from a streamlined flow, process ownership, and other impediments to lean. Deployment flowcharts show the procedural steps of a process along with who carries out each step. They combine the functions involved in the spaghetti flowchart with the sequencing steps used in logic flowcharting. Logic flowcharting is characterized by the use of symbols, as shown in exhibit 4-8. Logic flowcharts will be discussed in detail later in this chapter.

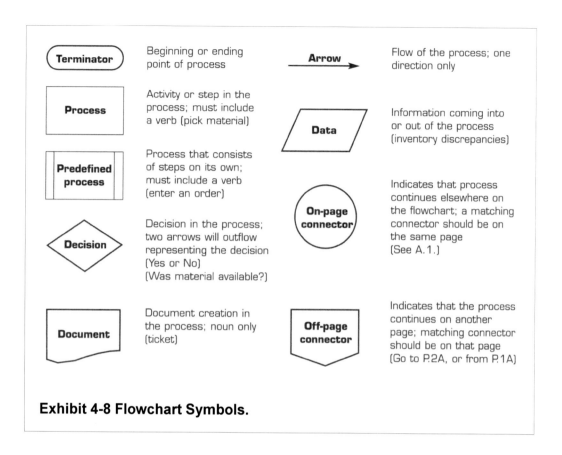

Exhibit 4-8 Flowchart Symbols.

Let's look at one electrical products distributor's deployment flowchart for order processing. The distributor began by identifying all of the activities and departments involved in the process. The activities are listed in the left-most column of a six-column chart and the departments are listed across the top of each column in "swim lanes" (exhibit 4-9).

Next, for each step, a flowchart symbol is placed in the swim lane of the function that performs the step (exhibit 4-10).

Functions / Activities	Warehouse	Inside Sales	Counter	Wire Cutting	Conduit Warehouse
Step 1: Identify functions and activities involved with the process					
1. START: Ticket prints					
2. Is ticket for wire cuts?					
3. Is ticket for conduit?					
4. Transfer ticket					
5. Order picking					
6. Check order					
7. Is order correct?					
8. Package and label order					
9. Locate wire					
10. Cut wire					
11. Label wire					
12. Locate conduit					
13. Bundle and label conduit					
14. Transfer to staging area					
15. Stage order for delivery					
END					

Exhibit 4-9 Deployment flowchart: Order production – Step 1.

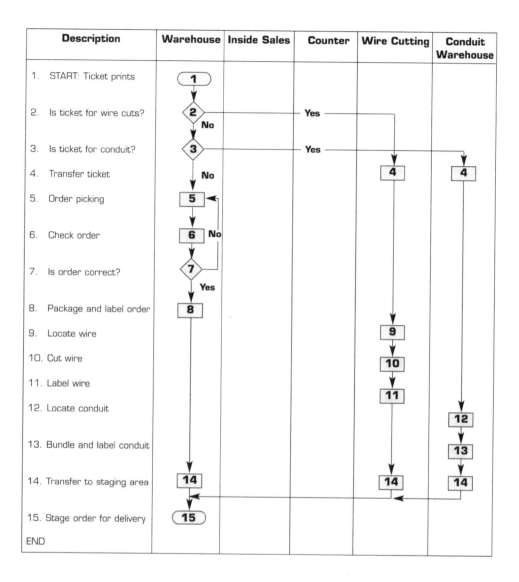

Description	Warehouse	Inside Sales	Counter	Wire Cutting	Conduit Warehouse
1. START: Ticket prints	1				
2. Is ticket for wire cuts?	2 / No		Yes		
3. Is ticket for conduit?	3		Yes		
4. Transfer ticket	No			4	4
5. Order picking	5				
6. Check order	6 No				
7. Is order correct?	7 / Yes				
8. Package and label order	8				
9. Locate wire				9	
10. Cut wire				10	
11. Label wire				11	
12. Locate conduit					12
13. Bundle and label conduit					13
14. Transfer to staging area	14			14	14
15. Stage order for delivery	15				
END					

Exhibit 4-10 Deployment flowchart: Order production – Step 2.

Once the causes of rework, waste, and errors have been made visible and their impact on other areas of the company understood (shown in this example by the sheer number of steps and the lines of request going in and out of them), the distributor's cross-functional team can develop a focused plan to target the systematic issues with full knowledge of how they affect each department in the company. For example, a change in the warehouse can easily require a change in the order-entry system, whether intentional or not.

Plan-Do-Study-Act (PDSA) cycles begin at this stage with a clearly defined statement of the issue and a proposed plan to target it. PDSA cycles involve planning for a change to the identified problem, testing (doing) the proposed change, comparing (studying) the test results to the existing process, and then acting on the results of the comparison. PDSA cycles are described below, and more details are provided in appendix C.

Characterize: Measure and Synthesize

A critical part of lean implementation is verification of improvement due to process redesign. In other words, is this process change an improvement over what I had before? The characterization stage of the SBPI® process brings in measurements and analysis, seeking to validate the issues you've identified for improvement. Are they real or perceived? How big is the opportunity for improvement in terms of capability, throughput, productivity, or cost? What is the potential financial impact?

The PDSA cycle begins here. An essential component is to develop how and where the problem will be objectively measured. As all improvements come through change--but by no means is every change an improvement--proposed process revisions must prove themselves on a small scale before being expanded or unilaterally adopted. Essentially, you must test your proposed changes.

In many cases, the initial problem being analyzed is often identified on a "gut feel" level—for example, it seems difficult, unwieldy, complicated, or excessive. Many of those instincts are correct, but they must be measured in order to provide a gauge by which to judge proposed changes. Some processes lend themselves to many different measures; successive PDSA cycles can focus on improving these one at a time until a test has fully been proven.

Measurements should always tie back to improved first-time pass, waste reduction, and improved customer point of entry. Some common measures among wholesale distribution companies are

- First-time pass yield
- Capability
- Cost
- System cycle time

- Takt time
- Fill rates
- Inventory discrepancies
- Back orders
- Picking errors
- Partial shipments
- Cancelled orders
- Shipping errors
- Billing errors
- Returns
- Late deliveries
- Expediting logs
- Inventory turns.

In many cases, the data on these issues are already available and captured in your system. In others, simple tally charts or daily logs are enough to get a general idea of the overall impact. For example, suppose the plan is to reduce partial shipments. One obvious measure is the number of partial shipments that go out in a typical week. You will use this data as a benchmark to test suggested changes to your shipping process.

 Comparing the data collected during the test to the data from measurements taken before the test will objectively show what has changed (if anything). For example, if the baseline measure of partial shipments before a test was 25 out of 100 shipments, the data will show whether the tested change resulted in fewer or more partial shipments.

Although PDSA cycles are designed to be run in quick, short increments, it is important to recognize that the test is being run in an artificial environment. The people carrying out a new procedure not only need time to learn the new procedure, but, in many cases, they must test the new one without giving up the old one. It may make for short-term extra work. The first set of measures show an increase as people adjust before stabilizing to the improvement level after the learning cycle has been further developed or even completed.

The intention, however, is to keep the cycles short term and focused—for example, you can use a test to find out if the information gathered on a proposed new order-entry form really is the correct information before applying resources to develop the process for using the form. You could test this by varying some of the input factors to see if the outcome changes. The initial PDSA cycles are learning tools. The concept must be proven first: Are we doing the right thing before considering whether we are doing it correctly?

A number of statistical tools can be used to analyze the information gathered from

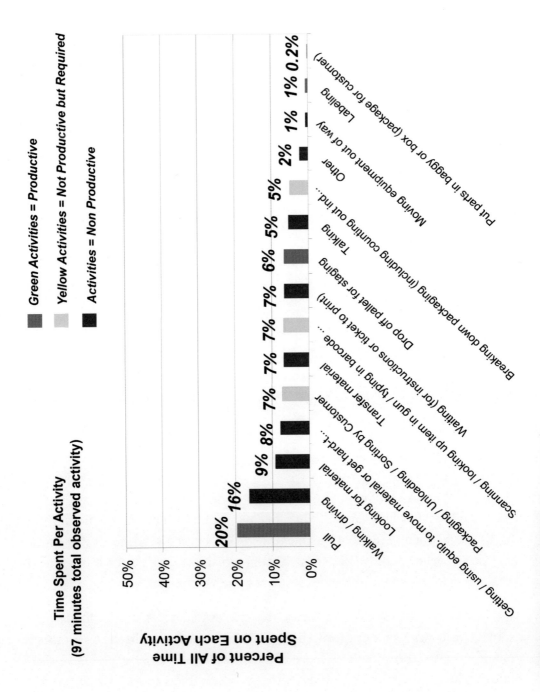

Exhibit 4-11 Picking Activity example.

the test. Some of the most powerful are Pareto charts, time lines, and run charts, snapshots of which are provided in the examples below. Pareto charts are bar charts organized from highest to lowest, allowing comparisons of data across categories in a single snapshot format. Exhibit 4-11 shows one distributor's analysis of time spent on picking activities, for example.

Time lines allow for measurements of value-added time or identification of staging time or downtime between steps. These flowcharts are powerful ways of identifying waste and first-time pass measures within a process. They begin with a terminator "start" symbol. Next, the steps of the process are identified and drawn in sequential order over time. The processing time (or effort) for each step, the total duration of each step, as well as the wait time in between are identified, and the steps on the chart are scaled accordingly (exhibit 4-12). Steps are coded as value-added or non-value-added, and wait time is always considered non-value-added. The percentage of non-value-added and value-added time is shown on the time line chart.

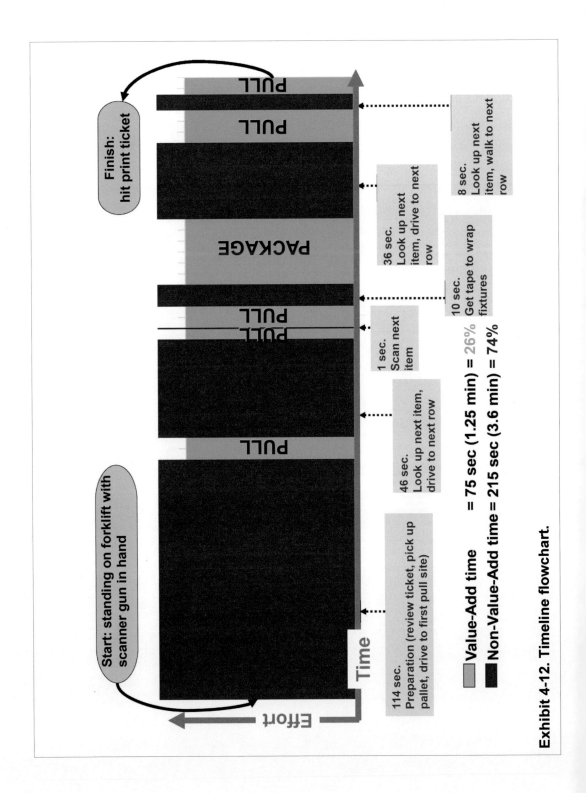

Exhibit 4-12. Timeline flowchart.

Run charts can be used to identify trends over time as well as to distinguish between special cause (outside influence) and common cause (process level) variation through the application of Statistical Process Control (SPC is a method for monitoring a process through the use of control charts. See the glossary for a detailed definition of SPC). Exhibit 4-13 shows a run chart of the cycle time needed to pick an individual ticket in one warehouse. Prior to the test, this distributor required 4.4 minutes per ticket, on average. The trend on the chart shows that a 1-week test led to a decrease in the average pick time to 3.94 minutes; the second week shows continuing improvement to an average of 3.4 minutes per ticket, which is continuing to decrease over time with the change in place. This 2-week test translated to a capability increase from 13.6 orders per hour and per warehouse picker to 17.6 orders per hour, almost a 30% increase with no additional personnel.

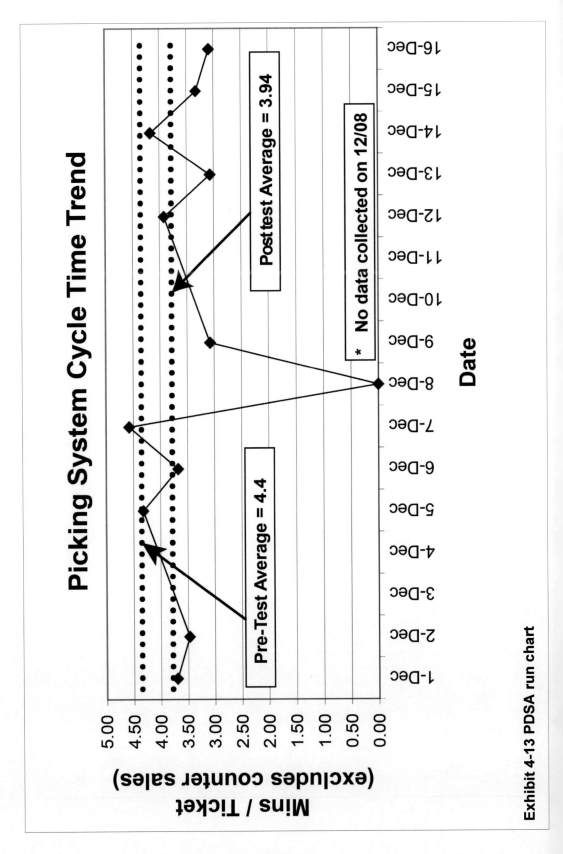

Picking System Cycle Time Trend

Posttest Average = 3.94

Pre-Test Average = 4.4

* No data collected on 12/08

Mins / Ticket (excludes counter sales)

Date

Exhibit 4-13 PDSA run chart

Of course, data must be taken in context. Raw numbers may be misleading, especially in seasonal or cyclical businesses. For example, a 20% increase in shipping errors by number during a period where the number of shipments doubled may well be an improvement on the originally identified problem or issue. The additional increase may suggest there is another factor that needs to be related and involved in the test during the next cycle. Distributors can then revisit their original fishbone diagram, spaghetti chart, and deployment flowchart to determine what that factor might be.

In addition, the data must be synthesized—that is, looked at in the context of the entire company. Increasing warehouse capability beyond that which can be sustained by the sales force introduces a different element of waste: overcapacity. However, the now additional resources are freed to address other needs throughout the company, perhaps even supplementing the sales force to take advantage of the new capacity.

The decision to accept or reject a proposed change based on hard experimental facts and data is the culmination of the PDSA cycle. Did this tested change result in improvement or not? Every improvement comes through a change, but not every change will be an improvement. The basic philosophy behind the PDSA cycle is that every proposed change is objectively tested to verify improvement. The purpose of the PDSA cycle is not to implement a change; rather it is to test a change on a small scale before rolling it out throughout the entire organization.

Applying PDSA cycles to test hunches, gut feelings, and points of distress in the workflow very often result in disproving those subjective expectations. It's not unusual to see failure in 25% to 50% of the tests—which by itself is an important tool for verifying an inappropriate hunch.

Finally, when analyzing PDSA cycle tests, you must consider the Hawthorne Effect. This occurs when people involved in a research study temporarily change their behavior or performance as a result of the observation rather than the actual test. The effect is named for the Hawthorne Works--a large factory complex in Illinois that operated from 1905 to 1983—where one study in a series of experiments on factory workers investigated the effect of lighting on workers' productivity. Researchers found that productivity almost always increased after a change in illumination, no matter what the level of illumination was—leading to the conclusion that it was the experience of being in a test that affected the results.

To avoid the Hawthorne Effect, you must design and implement a change management process; this will ensure that only the most significant changes (those that will lead to lasting improvements) are selected and institutionalized.

Optimize: Improve and Manage

The optimization stage of SBPI® is one of the most critical stages in the application of lean, because it includes designing for improved management of the changed processes.

Based on the test concept and design criteria, a pilot will be selected and designed. Once proposed changes have been tested, the successful elements can be selected and pulled together into a unified pilot design. At this point, the concept is put under stress: Can it withstand full-scale operations? Do negative effects appear or overwhelm the system with additional volume? A test that showed promise on a small scale may need additional support or infrastructure before it can be implemented on a larger scale.

Once a concept has been proven on a small scale, successful tests are put under stress in larger pilots before a major redesign of the process is implemented.

For example, several distributors have found through initial PDSA tests that locating the most frequently pulled items in a "quick pull" area of their warehouse vastly increased their warehouse's picking capacity. The pilots that followed at each company varied: In one location, the pilot was a target-circle layout with higher pulled items near the center and less frequently pulled items out along spokes. Another distributor's pilot was to collocate frequent items for specific large customers in "cells." A third distributor found that high-pick items often had related "go-with" items that also needed to be collocated in order to take full advantage of the area, and yet another distributor found that the system was best for short tickets and segregated its ticket-pulling assignments to quick-pull only and quick-pull plus.

The pilot plan is defined, tested, and carried out using the same process as the original PDSA cycle, beginning with defining the expected result, providing a specific description of the pilot and its parameters (who is involved, when, for how long, and so forth), and detailing the measurements that will be used to evaluate the pilot and the criteria to judge its success. If the pilot is a success, your team needs approval from management to implement the change across the entire wholesale distribution organization. The authorization request must be supported by documentation done at each step of the PDSA cycle and pilot tests, showing a demonstrable effect on the bottom line.

Support processes are not an important consideration in the testing phase. However, once the pilot has proven itself and has been approved for implementation, it can only be expanded on if it has been designed correctly with the appropriate support. The implementation design should include new process maps to show the flow and structure of the proposed implementation. Earlier maps would have shown "current state." At this point, logic flowcharts can be introduced to make the new design visible, including the underlying structure and how to address exceptions.

As explained in the Identify: Recognize and Define section earlier, logic flowcharts show the sequence of steps in a process and use the symbols shown in exhibit 4-8 to represent the activities involved. For example, a terminator shape indicates where a logic flowchart begins. Once the terminator is in place, each step is then drawn with the appropriate shape, in sequential order with the current logic of the process. All decision outcomes are shown in the form of branches. The logic flowchart flows forward and backward; that is, the flowchart shows all of the requirements for the process to go from start to finish and it also shows what the required inputs are for each step. Exhibit 4-14 is a sample flowchart for a distributor's receiving process.

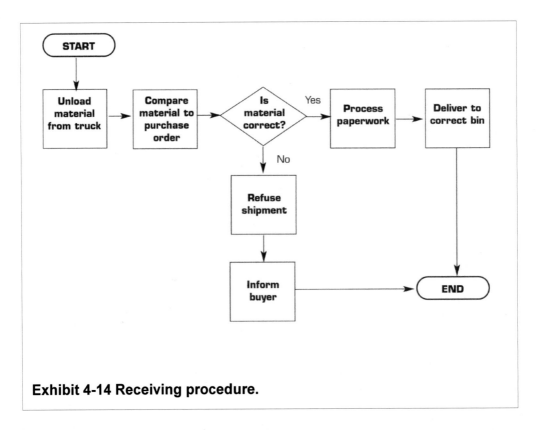

Exhibit 4-14 Receiving procedure.

The expansion plan for the pilot must also include the communication plan for the new design. How will we communicate the change? What information must be shared? In what format? The testing team is often in full support of the change initiatives, as they understand the development of the pilot and can predict the ripple effects. They also have the background knowledge of the test results and how it impacted each area. In other words, their own hesitations have been addressed.

Resistance to change becomes a critical factor in implementation; the rest of your employees must come to the same level of understanding through training, education, and well-founded trust that poor concepts have been eliminated prior to implementation. If the plan is not communicated effectively—with buy-in and understanding from everyone involved, however peripherally—implementation may still fail, even if the pilot was successful.

Unlike the test and development phases of new processes for lean, full implementation and application across your organization requires much more rigidity and structure. The progress must be continually measured. As explained in chapter 3, CPAC® is one measurement tool; it is able to combine the operational and financial aspects, as well as break down components and show developing trends.

As many companies use a multifaceted approach to identify and target their major waste and rework problems simultaneously, a visible dashboard or Enterprise Resource Planning (ERP) system can be used to keep changes and measurements visible and easily monitored. The dashboard or ERP system should show all critical measures of the system:

- A definition or description of each measure
- Scope of the measure
- Graphics: charts or tables (with clear descriptions and labels)
- Target performance levels
- Measurement "owner" (person who keeps and updates the data)
- Last update or revision date
- Data collection and reporting cycles.

Project plans can also be used to track the pilot and actual implementation of the new design. The plan serves as a visible means of communicating the scope and outcome of the project and includes a schedule, list of manageable tasks, and log of reported progress.

Quality Control

Any mechanical, electrical, or biological product requires some kind of maintenance to operate optimally and continuously. The best kind of maintenance is not repair, but preventive care. Distribution processes are not much different. They require constant maintenance to operate at their optimum output. A quality circle is a structured approach to maintenance of a system, and it also acts as a vehicle for continuous learning.

In a wholesale distribution environment, the quality circle is a cross-functional team of employees that focuses on optimizing the system for various activities, recognizing that correct, timely delivery to the customer is the ultimate goal.

The institutionalization of lean carries unique risks. If not managed correctly, any of the following can turn into major pitfalls during the implementation phase. The top implementation risks are

- Lack of management support
- Lack of management understanding
- Lack of available resources
- Lack of correct training
- Personnel shifts
- Lack of buy-in
- Mismatch of risk or rewards with the new process.

Risk management must be an integral part of your overall approach to change management. Therefore, risk identification must be part of your implementation plan. By careful management to reduce the unknown or uncertain elements and increase the known facts of the situation, risk can be mitigated, if not avoided. To do this, constant feedback is required from all stakeholders—customers, vendors, management, order-processing workers, salespeople, and back-office personnel—and an efficient issue-resolution process should be put in place.

Utilize: Standardize and Integrate

Overall recognition and acceptance of the new process will only come when the results speak for themselves and do not need any interpretation. Designed changes are sustainable only when they are fully incorporated. Lean operations must become a part of daily business.

The next step in the SBPI® process is to institutionalize the concepts, taking change management to an enterprise wide strategy focused on learning and translating changes into sustainable improvements in terms of time, cost, and quality. The SBPI® process and the fact-based learning culture it supports must constantly and consistently run in the background of the entire system.

The popular term "standard work" is often used to describe the utilization stage (see the glossary for more information). Essentially, the final stage of the SBPI® process results in processes that are done the same way each and every time.

The next chapter describes how a national distributor used the SBPI® process to implement lean.

CHAPTER 5

Real-World Example: National Distributor

The example here and those in Chapters 6 and 7 show how a national, regional, and local distributor have used the SBPI® process, explained in chapter 4, to implement lean in their companies. Each example describes the overarching problem the wholesaler-distributor faced and the steps the company took to analyze, test, and implement changes necessary to make improvements.

The examples were selected to demonstrate the ease or difficulties involved in applying lean due to geographical, cultural, and political environments governing various types of organizations.

IMPLEMENTING SBPI®

Every day wholesaler-distributors face the question: Who are we? Are we our manufacturers' distributors or our customers' suppliers?

Why is it so difficult to answer this question? The distribution industry is facing a shift across the entire industry. Manufacturers and end users are circumnavigating distributors in some cases, buying and selling directly, and in bulk, and acting in direct competition to their traditional distributors. Material purchasing by third-party brokers does not help the situation from the distributor's cost and profit perspective.

A national distributor (ND) with branches spread all over the country was looking for solutions to adapt to the current market conditions. The distributor decided to implement lean, based on customer demand and the dynamics of the changing marketplace, and began by asking the following questions:

1. Distributors and suppliers have different needs: What are they?

2. Manufacturers and retailers also have different requirements: What are those requirements?

3. Underlying operations and cost drivers are different among distributors, manufacturers, retailers, and customers.

   a. What are their cost drivers? How are they different?

   b. How do these differences impact the distributor's operation?

4. How should distributors structure their companies? What strategies are needed to support the contradictory and opposing needs of their core stakeholders and constituencies? Is partnership a viable option? If so, with whom: Manufacturers, retailers or customers?

To answer these questions, ND tried servicing the customer through integrated supply partnerships and quickly recognized the shortcomings of its current support process—one of which was a lack of understanding the customer's needs. The ND improvement process started with showing its associates how to understand the customer and how to become better service providers.

ND started by changing its existing operational philosophy from being a *distributor* to being a *supplier*—connecting customers with their needed material. In a brainstorming session at the executive level, ND had recognized that traditional distributors provide services to customers as "add-ons" to their existing business model; essentially, they partner on the supply side and push material through the chain. They realized that suppliers, on the other hand, partner with the demand side—with customers. Suppliers provide services in addition to just selling material—services that are integrated into their offerings alongside their product lines.

To support the customer's need for services, ND had added service activities to its current distribution model, but was unable to sustain its traditional profitability levels because those services were not part of an existing system. ND decided to hire MCA, Inc. to help transform the company from a *distributor* into a *supplier*.

SBPI® was used to redesign, test, and implement processes that would take ND from being a distributor with add-on services to being a supplier with cost-effective services that customers perceived as value-added. The goal was to transform the company into a lean organization with top-notch customer service.

Due to the enormous size of the company, the executives decided to use the company's eastern region as a pilot.

Initiative Start-up

A steering committee was formed at the executive level to oversee the SBPI® activities. The steering committee selected corporate-level managers as initiative leaders and allowed them to identify the local-level team members as participants. A 2 ½-day off-site meeting was arranged to gather all team members for the initiative start-up. What follows are the excerpts from ND's team reports for 2 years of testing, piloting, implementing, and institutionalizing the lean process through SBPI®.

Initial Off-Site Workshop

In order to be able to measure the progress of the lean initiative, some baseline operational paradigms and performance measures had to be established. The team identified the following bottlenecks, problems, and frustrations as obstacles to achieving a lean distributorship with excellent customer service:

- Nobody takes responsibility/ownership/accountability
- Lack of data
- Financial limitations
- Lack of continuous improvement/training
- Inadequate staffing/insufficient staffing
- Internal promotion/limited "promote-able" people
- Too much change at once
- ERP system
- We confuse our customers
- Lack of involvement.

The team identified the following areas as opportunities for improvement:

- Flexibility
- Partnering
- Error Reduction
- Value-added services
- Reliability/follow-through
- Listening to the customer
- Better communication
- Attention to detail
- Thinking outside the box.

The team then identified these cost drivers of the distributor's operations: orders, invoices, line items, billing corrections, shipments in, shipments out, quotation errors, job-site visits, deliveries, returns, selection errors, and necessary approvals.

Consequently, order entry was identified as a very costly process and the team used a fishbone diagram (exhibit 5-1) to uncover the root causes of the costs. Under the categories of material, facilities, people, process, and technology, the process and people "legs" on the diagram carried the heaviest weight, which meant they should be addressed first.

Agile Distribution®

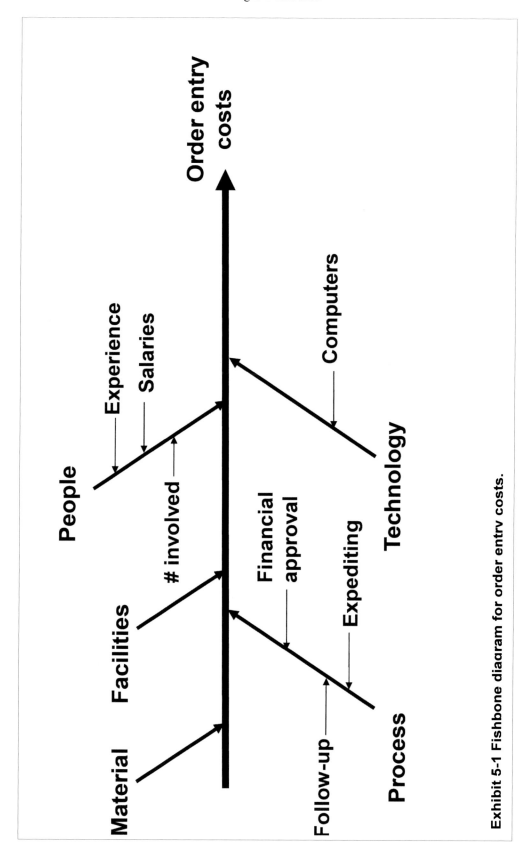

Exhibit 5-1 Fishbone diagram for order entry costs.

87

Customer Point of Entry (CPE)

Every customer enters your order process from one of several portals—outside sales, inside sales, the counter, Internet, catalog, or USPS mail. But the customer's point of entry shouldn't be limited to these portals, since once he is at the portal, he's already made up his mind about the purchase, service, delivery, and so on. Distributors with this operational model are at a disadvantage because they are reacting to the customer's needs. A more innovative portal for customer entry into your system is reconnaissance-based customer data gathering. In other words, you must create early warning signals of customer behavior that will allow your system to operate leaner.

In looking at our example, ND realized it was in a reactive mode. Customers' "right-now" demands had caused ND to stockpile massive inventories to ensure it met those demands. Rush service includes costs associated with carrying inventory, unavailable capital allocated to inventory, and zone warehousing. Customer requirements for reliability and cash-flow management also encourage customers to order large quantities of material at the beginning of a season to earn bulk discounts or ensure material is not back-ordered when it is needed. This material often sits in their inventory until the end of their fiscal year when customers return a large amount of the inventory to the distributor, causing a surge of rework in addition to tying up resources.

During ND's off-site session, the team recognized that customers' needs were unknown to them and that they did not have an early-warning signal for customers' buying habits. One strategy to reduce the costs associated with carrying inventory and inventory returns—to both ND and its customers—is building partnerships that feature higher frequency and richness of communication and early warning signals. Many of those inventory costs can be reduced simply by understanding each other's true needs. However, each party needs to understand how the other makes its money.

Game Theory

As explained in chapter 4, Game Theory applies to the analysis of conflict situations and corresponding strategies for decision making. ND team members were introduced to Game Theory to further their understanding of the conflicting interests of various departments within the wholesaler-distributor and among partners in the supply chain. Game Theory explains that there is always a "best" solution, though that solution may not always seem best for any one player, company, or department. Rather, the best solution is the one that benefits all players in the game. There are five PARTS to every game:

- **P**layers: Individuals or groups with interest in the game
- **A**dded Value: The value brought by each player
- **R**ules: The regulations or conventions followed
- **T**actics: The strategies employed by players
- **S**cope: The boundaries of the game.

A change to any one of those parts will change the game—and the solution. To manage even the basic game consisting of a single transaction, ND needed to consider the effects of every one of the subgames or strategies being employed anywhere in the cycle.

The team members brainstormed and realized that their interactions involved many players, both directly and indirectly. Exhibit 5-2 shows the team members' breakdown of various functions involved in their game from a customer's perspective. In order to get material from ND's warehouse, a customer may have dealt with many different divisions at ND. In addition, the customer was trying to balance ND's requirements with the demands and requirements placed on him by his own internal company processes and those imposed by his external business relationships.

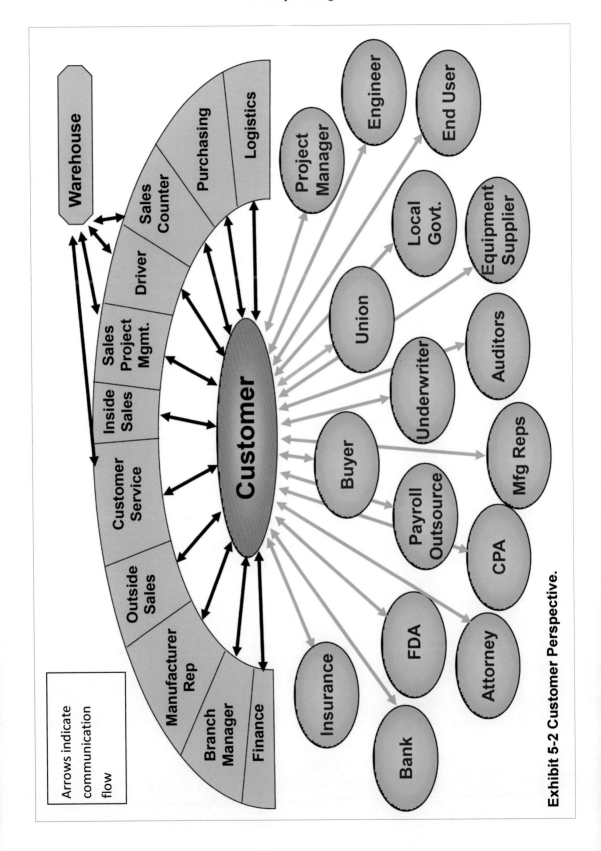

Exhibit 5-2 Customer Perspective.

Sales, Production, and Service

ND has three major areas of operation: sales, production, and service. Sales is the traditional portal of customer entry into the company. ND has outside sales, which are mainly commission-based positions. Outside sales associates are after large sales and contracts. Their primary function is generation of sales and customer contact. The inside sales or customer care function is primarily responsible for order taking and follow-up with all customer orders. Once the orders have been placed by the inside sales group, the job of the order processing group starts. Dropping the ticket in the warehouse is the trigger for the pick, pack, and ship operation. Putting the orders on the trucks for delivery triggers the service group's activities. From delivery to returns to customer orders, follow-up is the service group's responsibility. As part of MCA, Inc.'s operation assessment, the current flow of operations among these three groups and their customers is shown in exhibit 5-3. The exhibit reveals that there is no direct communication between ND's sales department and the actual user (the supervisors/end users) of the product or service.

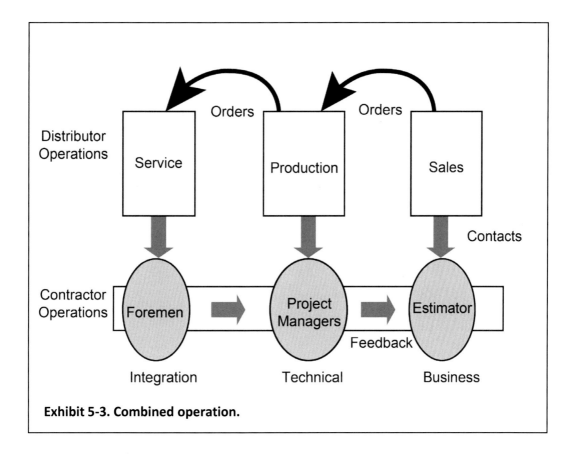

Exhibit 5-3. Combined operation.

After the team reviewed the workflow, it was obvious that these three areas needed to cooperate and work toward a common goal, with complete flow of information. These areas needed to be part of the same game, working cooperatively to arrive at the best outcome throughout the entire process.

As the team expanded its view of each area and considered the larger game, they identified the players, the added values brought by the various players, the rules being played by (or who was making the rules), the tactics, and the scope of the process that applied to the project they were examining. Exhibit 5-4 summarizes the team's input about players, added value, rules, tactics, and scope for sales, service. and order processing.

	Sales	Order Processing	Service
Players	Sales reps Buyers Manufacturer Customer Competition Management	Order entry Inside sales Pick-pack-ship Inspection Receiving/Shipping Returned goods Drivers	Warehouse Our drivers Third-party drivers All sales and production players Receptionist Factories
Added Value	Interpret customer expectations Product knowledge and training Financing Customer cost savings Storage On-time delivery No partial deliveries Personal relationship with sales rep Project management	Honest expectations Reduction of errors Shipment notification Special handling requirements Expediting Staging Project management	Effective communication of customer needs/ of delivery expectations Preassembly Onsite material handling Kitting Labeling/Packaging Summary billing Returns
Rules	Partnering versus traditional distributorship Identify customer needs Price flexibility On-time quotes and feedback Part numbers/description Accurate billing Financial terms	Open communication—internal and external Accurate delivery Accurate pick-pack-ship Single point of contact to national distributor	Consistency Communication Underpromise/Overdeliver Timeliness Accuracy Follow-up
Tactics	Find the decision maker Understand customer rules/influences Price flexibility Supplier selection Partnering Quoting Inventory deployment Using technology Differentiation	Use of technology Checking process Warehouse layout Information to and from sales Handling returns	Good communication Uncover customer needs Quality products Turn negatives into positives
Scope	Order size Delivery requirements Product availability	Type of material Customer requirements Length of engagement with customer	24/7 availability Local availability Service multiple customers

Exhibit 5-4. Workflow evaluation

The team then formed design teams for each of the company's three operational areas. Cross-functionality of the design teams is a critical aspect of lean application. It is vital that each design team has a representative from various segments of the company. The members of ND's lean design teams for sales, order processing, and service were selected from various functions in the organization. The functions represented on each team were:

Cross-functional Design Teams

Sales Team

Leader: Inside Sales Manager

Team: Checker, Truck Driver, Credit, Order Entry, Buyer, Ticket Logger

Service Team

Leader: Shipping Supervisor

Team: Inside Salesperson, Receptionist, Accounts Receivable, Picker, Account Manager, Special Services Manager

Order Processing Team

Co-leaders: Warehouse Manager

Team: Receiving Associate, Outside Salesperson, Driver, Purchasing Manager, Returned Goods, Pick-Pack-Ship Supervisor

A separate core team was established to reduce the steering committee's workload at the operational level. The core team--led by ND's COO and consisting of the team leaders—managed the gaps, overlaps and flow of information among the design teams.

Following the SBPI® process, the design teams were asked to brainstorm and identify the top issues under the distributor's categories of first-time pass, waste reduction, and customer point of entry. With this information, the teams could come up with a plan to gather baseline data for the design of their first PDSAs. The teams identified the following issues under each category and for each segment of the operations:

Sales Team

First-Time Pass

- Accurate information
- Complete information
- Correct quantity
- Right cost
- Communication of customer delivery expectations

Reduction of Waste

- Complete information
- Correct quantities
- Correct price
- Correct "ship to" address and contact information
- Identification of customer needs

Customer Point of Entry

- Estimators (employees who estimate the value of a project in order to win a bid)
- Project managers should be involved as soon as possible
- Not enough information on when/where/who to deliver
- Foreman involved as early as possible
- Incomplete order information

Service Team

First-Time Pass

- Accuracy
- Reduce selection errors
- Answer the phone in a timely manner
- Respond to customer's special requests
- Identify special requirements

Reduction of Waste

- Correct Pricing
- Accurate selection
- Rework
- Effects of correct data
- Have correct data/information in ERP system

Customer Point of Entry

- Order packaging method based on customer request
- Communicate
- Emergencies due to poor planning
- Order time line/delivery dates
- Reliability and consistency for accuracy

Order Processing Team

First-Time Pass

- Accurate pick/pack/ship
- Accurate billing
- Accurate order entry
- Fill rate
- Releasing on time

Reduction of Waste

- Garbage in--Garbage out
- Have correct inventory available
- Price correctly for the customer
- Determine customer's needs
- Deliver the total order

Customer Point of Entry

- Everyone communicate
- Own the request until the customer is satisfied
- Everyone respond to customer
- Connect customer to proper person
- Quick response

For the next 30 days, the three design teams collected data on these issues and tracked their progress to report to the core team. The data collection plan was developed for each team as shown below:

Sales Team:

- Flowchart processes
- Track/collect data
- Track problems
- Identify stock/commodity issues

Service Team:

First-Time Pass

- Identify the current situation
- Measure accuracy
- Research other models
- Identify desired future state
- Identify special requirements

Reduce Waste

- Measure first-time pass
- Identify greatest contributors to rework

Customer Point of Entry

- Investigate current communication situation
- Measure impact of poor planning

Order Processing Team:

First-Time Pass

- Interview
- Measure
- Determine available data

Waste Reduction

- Apply data from first-time pass to waste reduction
- Interview involved participants in the process
- Create list of interview questions

Customer Point of Entry

- Identify current levels of communication
- Identify areas of communication breakdown
- Measure frequency of communication
- Investigate feedback measures

Application and Institutionalization of Lean Approach

ND's lean design teams used the SBPI® approach and identified many opportunities to use the PDSA to develop tests and proofs of concepts. Subsequently, the teams selected a few successful test results and elevated them to regional pilot programs. Once the pilots were proven to have the expected outcome of improved productivity and throughput, they were then applied downstream to customer service, and upstream to the manufacturer's delivery process. What follows are two examples of how ND applied these lean strategies on both sides of the supply chain:

Customer Application

ND's application of lean with their customer started with a full-service vendor-partner model. After a year of design and application of a partnership with a key customer, ND saw an increase in overall company sales by 30%. ND also uncovered a new business opportunity through servicing the customer and increased sales within a small niche market by more than 70%.

Major accomplishments included:

- Summary billing implemented for all transactions
- Buyback of inventory stored at the customer of more than $50,000
- Customer site visits to learn about its operation and cost drivers
- Point-to-point delivery at customer's specification (not just at the dock doors)
- Storage of "big buy" items for the customer, with specified delivery release dates
- Expansion of partnership pilot to two other key customers
- EDI exchanges—ND's pricing structure was integrated with the customer's ERP system and updated monthly
- Issue resolution put in place to identify and solve concerns together, as partners.

Supplier Application

Once the application of lean and its advantages were established both by internal improvements at ND and at the customer level with that particular key customer, the process was expanded to ND's suppliers to improve the flow of goods all the way from the manufacturer to the user. One of ND's main equipment manufacturers was selected to be part of the lean chain. ND requested that the manufacturer visit the key customer at its operation level. After that visit and a few brainstorming sessions, the manufacturer understood how it could better service ND and the customer. The manufacturer identified several opportunities for product improvement and discovered areas where it could improve service delivery, including:

- Web-based tools to help the customer with new product information and inventory checking
- Dealing with damage caused by carriers
- Packing product so that all labels are visible to make it easy to validate orders upon receipt

- Training on product awareness
- Training on application of tools (that is, system productivity)

Lean Supply Chain

The combined efforts of distributor, customer, and supplier resulted in a list of services and information exchange that would reduce non-value-added activities, time, and variance in the entire chain. The list of improved activities included: Bar coding, kitting, technical assistance, training, on-site tool cribs, storeroom management, inventory reduction, bin restocking for service trucks, summary billing, consignment, EDI, electronic funds transfer, site surveys, among many others. These were things the partners could undertake to improve communication flow and drive efficiency in all three organizations.

In developing the partnership, the companies developed a "Vendor Partner Comment Card" that could be filled out by anyone (involved in all three companies), who observed an issue that he or she could not resolve alone, or that impacted multiple areas of the organization (exhibit 5-5).

Comment #:_____

Partner Submitting Comment:

Submitted by: _____   Phone Number: _____

Date Submitted: _____   Reported to: _____

Departments/Areas involved:

Category of Comment:

     ☐ Quote/Spec   ☐ Pricing   ☐ Wrong material   ☐ Delivery problem

     ☐ Timeliness   ☐ Communication   ☐ Accounting (billing/collecting)

Comments/Notes: _____

_____

_____

Frequency of occurrence: _____

Impact of occurrence:

Assigned to: Requested response date:

Investigation results: _____

_____

_____

Resolution: _____

_____

_____

Date: Responsible:

Exhibit 5-5. Vendor/Partner comment

HOW TO APPLY AT YOUR COMPANY

If you're a national distributor reading this, the key question becomes: How do I go about doing this at my company? As explained at the outset, lean is not something you should take on alone. It's important to get outside help. However, there are some things that you can do to prepare for your lean journey. You can start the SBPI® process (described in chapter 4 and elaborated in this chapter) by gathering your executive team for an initiative start-up. Talk about the key challenges your company is facing in the marketplace. Ask yourselves these general questions:

1. What is our company's mission?
2. What do our customers need?
3. Do we fully understand our customers' needs?
4. What are our needs?
5. What are our suppliers' needs?
6. How can we improve our supplier relationships to better serve our customers?
7. What obstacles do we face in achieving our mission and goals?

Then ask these specific questions:

1. How do we add value?
2. What is value from the customer's perspective?
3. What are the transactions in our processes that the customer does not know or care for?
4. How many transactions do we have to commit to before we satisfy customers' requests?
5. What is our first time pass?
6. Do we know our cost of processing orders?
7. What are the costs of errors in our system?
8. How do we lose customers?
9. How do we gain customers?
10. What is the cost of a lost customer?
11. What is the cost of carrying a customer?
12. What is our customer's point of entry into our system?

As a national distributor, you should choose a region or hub of your company to focus on before going any further. Remember, the SBPI® process is done on a small-scale basis first. Once you've done that, identify the employees you would select for a cross-functional team to address the issues you've identified. Then bring that team together and further brainstorm some issues.

Once your team is in place, you can walk through the eight key steps of the SBPI® process:

1. Prioritize your list of issues, then select the top issues to be addressed. Develop a plan for gathering data on those issues.

2. Select the issue you'll tackle first—the issue for which you'll develop a PDSA (Plan-Do-Study-Act cycle, also described in chapter 4). Then plan your tests.

3. Brainstorm about how you would perform the tests, collect the data, and resolve any issues that may arise.

4. Discuss how you would analyze the data, what criteria you would use for accepting a change to an existing process, and how you would select a pilot.

5. Talk about how you would evaluate the pilot, and how, if the pilot was successful, you would expand it into larger pilots.

6. Discuss the "dashboard" you would use to track the pilot; these are tools and measurements described in chapter 4. What information should you include in the dashboard? Also, decide who would be in your "quality circle"—the cross-functional team of employees charged with overseeing this particular process/system indefinitely.

7. Describe how you would test the proposed change(s) across the organization. Identify any risks and develop a plan to manage those risks.

8. Figure out how you would incorporate the change(s) in your company's regular operations. How would you communicate the change(s)—internally and externally to customers and suppliers?

CHAPTER 6

Real-World Example: Regional Distributor

A particular regional distributor (RD) operates with distribution centers in Georgia and Alabama. Those two hubs serve branches that operate in the Southeast, from Florida up to Tennessee. The distributor is very individual-customer oriented, even though it continues to expand geographically and financially. RD's culture is heavily focused on organizational learning, and the company has developed various types of performance measurements. RD has adopted a team-based approach to problem solving, and quality teams are already in place.

The executives at RD successfully trained their associates to diligently focus on measuring processes and to pay attention to quality. However, the working level of the organization (the "do-er bees") was only going through the motions of control charting and end-of-line inspection. They had no formalized system for making process changes and were missing the fundamental understanding of system design.

Because RD's historic attempt at continuous improvement had not penetrated the working levels of the company, the distributor hired MCA, Inc. to help further implement a lean strategy. Following the SBPI® steps, RD's steering committee included the company owners, who were familiar with the local operations. They developed a team charter for the distributor's Alabama operation as shown in exhibit 6-1.

General Description:

Operations is a process that starts with the initial order taking and processing. It continues with ticket drop in the warehouse, material positioned in the truck ready for delivery, and ends with delivery and positioning of the material at the customer-defined location. It is a series of contacts, decisions, and actions that begin with the earliest steps of order taking, order processing, ticket printing, picking, sorting, inspecting, loading, and delivery; it does not end until the material is at the customer-defined location, as needed according to what, where, and when was defined by the end user. It is completed when improvement lessons are captured and integrated into standard methods of doing business.

Expected Results:

- Map the process of operation starting with order taking
- Identify the potential activities that could be improved
- Suggest improvements and test on a small scale
- Confirmed improvements will have the following characteristics:
  —Improve the process by better than 30%
  —Reduce the cost of operation by better than 5%
  —Are sustainable
  —Are trainable
  —Can be used across the company with minimal adjustments.

Make significant movement toward accomplishing these objectives by fourth quarter.

Exhibit 6-1 Regional distributor team charter:

The distributor's steering committee formed a team of members from these functional areas:

- Operations Manager (team leader)
- Warehouse Manager
- Warehouse Assistant Manager
- Inventory Records Control Supervisor
- Receiving Supervisor
- Outside Salesman
- Inside Salesman
- Counter Salesman.

As with the previous national distributor example, RD's team members participated in an initial off-site meeting and brainstormed the process elements involved in sales, order processing, and service. The steering committee decided the focus of this lean project would be limited to order processing. The order processing activities were then broken down into order entry, ticket pulling, and receiving.

Process Mapping

The team began to make the processes visible by flowcharting the current situation in order entry, ticket pulling, and receiving. The flowcharts indicated that the processes could get cumbersome very quickly if there were any deviations from the "optimal" order flow. For example, exhibit 6-2 shows that receiving only involves two functions if there are no problems (the two functions are "Receiving Associate" and "UPS/Motor Freight" and they are listed along the top of the chart).

Steps	Customer	Inside Sales	Outside Sales	Counter Sales	Branch Mgr.	Sales Mgr.	J.D. Edwards	Vendor / Supplier	Prchsg./Buyer	Credit Dept.	SPA Dept.	Customer Serv. Super.	RG Dept.	IRC	Ticket Puller	Wire Dept.	Conduit Dept.	Check-Pack	QCS	Receiving Assoc.	Driver	UPS/Motor Frt.	Receiving Superv.
1. Material arrives																						Start → 1	
2. Validate counter is at the right address																						2	
3. Is it UPS?																						3 (Y)	
4. Is it wire, lamps, or fixtures?																				4 (Y/N)	N		
5. Offload & check (against packing slip) as offloading																				5			
6. Offload																				6	Y	6	
7. Check in against packing slip																				7			
8. Are there any problems with the material?																				8	Y		Go to P.3
9. Fix problems																							
10. Is it UPS?																				10 (N)			
11. Log in on manifest																				11 (Y)			
12. Receive online																				12			
13. Are there any problems?																				13 (N)	Y		Go to P.5
14. Fix problems																							
15. Print put away sheets for B/O tickets																				15 → 2			

Exhibit 6-2. Deployment Flowchart for Receiving.

However, when problems occur, the receiving process could involve more than 10 people to resolve the issues on hand. Based on the flowcharts, the team brainstormed and prioritized issues to address as shown in exhibit 6-3.

Order Entry	Total	Priority Minimum	Maximum
Sales/Order entry asking right questions of customer	52	3	10
Credit approval process for orders over $5,000	50	2	10
IMET material after 5:00 p.m.	39	1	9
SPAs: picked up in system, current, correct	42	3	8
Back-ordered items	67	3	10
Approval process for new suppliers	41	2	10
Follow-ups to make sure instructions are read and followed	41	2	9
Late delivery orders added in (holding up trucks)	52	5	8

Ticket Pulling	Total	Priority Minimum	Maximum
Load on customer service super	74	6	10
Material not in primary location	52	1	8
Product knowledge—location	59	2	10
Product knowledge—verification of material	66	2	10
Ticket changes at load out	52	5	10

Ticket Pulling—Truck Non-Bar Code	Total	Priority Minimum	Maximum
Pipe/Wire info on tickets (product knowledge; pull versus cut, correctly)	56	6	10
Items in primary location	48	1	8
Research: Was material received into the system?	52	7	9
Back order items not found	55	5	10

Receiving	Total	Priority Minimum	Maximum
Staging/Picking back orders	45	5	10
Research: Was material received into the system?	42	3	8
No packing slip at check-in	33	0	8
Incoming material damaged/freight claims	36	2	8
No purchase order to receive against	34	1	7
Receiving material intended for another branch/location	22	1	8
Receiving damaged material	24	1	6
Receiving incorrect quantities	38	0	7
Receiving incorrect items	30	0	7
Back order tickets not printed	54	5	10
Customer for back order on credit hold	36	2	9
Canceling lines	47	1	9
Reentering back-ordered lines (releasing back order)	62	6	10

Exhibit 6.3 Ranking issues.

Data Collection and Test Setup

The team adopted the Toyota Production System's method of continuous improvement for data gathering: *Genchi Genbutsu*, which means go see-for-yourself, was used to discover the activities involved in processing an order. Essentially, the team observed the order process from start to finish. Exhibit 6-4 shows what activities were observed during pulling tickets. Almost two-thirds of a puller's time was spent on non-value-added activities. The majority of that non-value-added time was spent walking or driving and looking for material because it was not in the correct location.

Consequently, a team was set up to improve the ordering process by reducing or eliminating the non-value-added and unnecessary activities of ticket pulling. The team discovered that if the two major categories of non-value-added activities were reduced—looking for material and walking/driving time as shown in exhibit 6-4—the calculated value for capacity improvement was an astonishing 21%. Exhibit 6-5 shows how the distributor arrived at this savings.

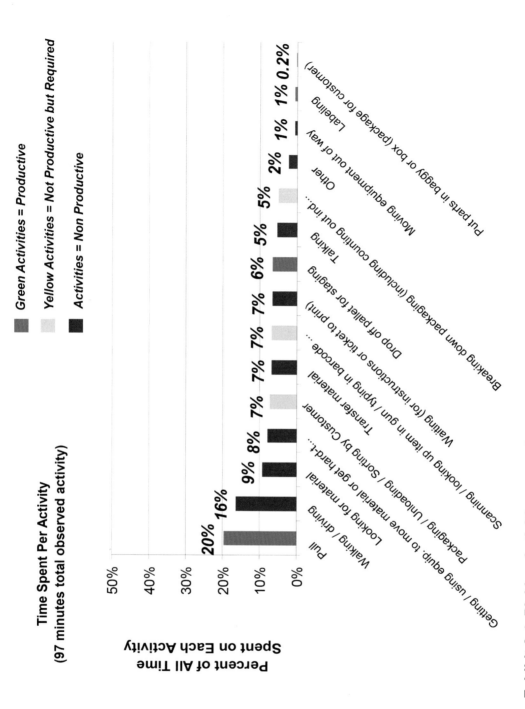

Exhibit 6-4. Picking Activities example.

	Current	Eliminate Looking for Material (9% of pulling time)	Reduce Walking/Driving by 10%	Do Both
Time to pull 1 line (minute/line)	0.92	0.92 − (0.92 x 9%) = 0.837	0.92 − (0.92 x 10%) = 0.828	
Capacity	1,750	(0.92 x 1,750) ÷ 0.837 = 1,923 lines	(0.92 x 1,750) ÷ 0.828 = 1,944 lines	1,923 − 1,750 = 173 1,944 − 1,750 = 194 1,750 + 173 + 194 = 2,117 lines
Revenue dollars (based on $50/line and 360 working days/year)	1,750 x $50 x 360 = $31.5M	1,923 x $50 x 360 = $34.6M	1,944 x $50 x 360 = $35.0M	2,117 x $50 x 360 = $38.1 M
Profit dollars (based on 16% gross margin)	$5.0M	$5.5M	$5.6M	$6.1 M

Exhibit 6-5 Capacity improvement

To eliminate looking for material, the team initially proposed increasing inventory levels. The thought behind this hypothesis was that if there was more inventory, RD would never run out and the pickers would always be able to pull what they needed for the customer's order. However, increasing inventory is very expensive and would not solve the problem of non-value-added activities. So, the issue was revisited from a different angle. A question was posed to the team that clarified the underlying root cause: Was it the quantities of material that would reduce the problem of looking for material or was it the material availability? The team concluded that it was the latter and then set out to discover how to increase the material availability without increasing the inventories.

One of the issues impacting product availability was the process of receiving. The team discovered that even if the material was physically available, the receiving of the product electronically and its put away was not a priority. This is because the receiving function typically did not fall under daily "firefighting" duties.. Therefore, material could have been available for pulling if it was received in a timely manner.

In essence, for product to be available sooner, it would need to be put away sooner. For example, if a salesperson ordered an item, it may show up as available because it had been "received online" (recognized as received inside RD's ERP system); however, the product may not have been "physically received" (put away) yet. This means that the item ordered by the salesperson is not available for the picker to pull, and this causes a back order.

To tackle this issue, the team designed a PDSA test for a new receiving process in which the material was not received online until it was physically put away.

The distributor's Georgia warehouse had developed a similar process using the SBPI® method. The order processing team studied the Georgia receiving process and planned a test for that process on incoming material from four different suppliers. The Georgia process was tweaked slightly for the Alabama operations' setup. The existing process in Alabama split the duties with associates, using two separate crews for receiving and put away. The test process split the duties by the type of incoming delivery—freight, courier, and inter-company (branch) deliveries—rather than by crew. The associate who unloads the truck is the same person who follows the material all the way through to putting it on the shelf.

Running the Tests

The receiving PDSA ran for 1 week and the order processing team measured at least a 1-hour improvement in the material availability time. In the redesigned process all shipments were unloaded and put away within an hour of arrival, whereas it took an average of 3 hours for material to be available prior to the test.

The team also saw a reduction in time spent looking for material during pulling by 7% to 8% within a month of the test as shown in exhibit 6-6.

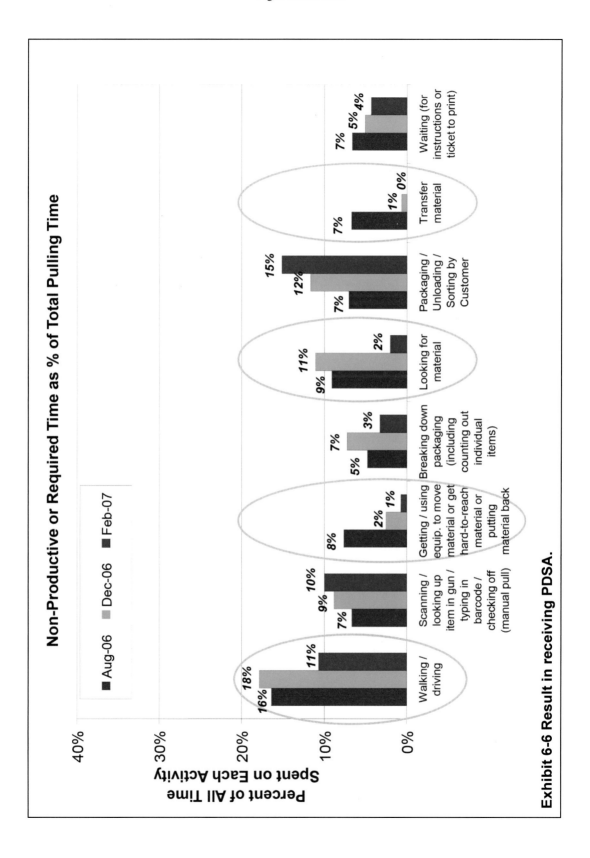

Exhibit 6-6 Result in receiving PDSA.

Application of Accepted Tests

The team continued to test the receiving process and accepted the test as successful. The team was ready to expand on the concept of the receiving process, and developed a PDSA test to gauge whether or not product is available for pulling as soon as it is demanded.

The next step was to develop a pilot for one of the successful PDSAs—the successfully redesigned receiving process above, for example. The pilot would stress the new design on a small scale before rolling it out companywide. Meanwhile, the continuous improvement process went on. RD's design team formed new teams to address other issues within the division; the new teams reported back to the original design team. The predicted savings and increased profitability of the design team's activities for this regional distributor is in millions of dollars in annual terms.

Prior to applying the pilot, RD's original design team was asked to develop a list of issues, based on their experience with SBPI® and the lean process, which would be passed on to the next team members. Some of their comments included:

- Make results from other impacted groups visible and anecdotal
- Understand what we are trying to accomplish
    o What's the benefit?
    o What's in it for the employees?
    o What's in it for the company?
- Teach the team the process—the philosophy behind it
- Give clear definitions, assignments and expectations
- Explain the reasons for lean—we're not trying to eliminate people, we're trying to make them more productive
- Ask for ideas from people closest to the job—get their input, buy-in, and fingerprint
- Improve the relationships among departments
- Reduce the finger-pointing
- Know that the changes will be improvements
    o Have confidence in the system—that what is said will actually happen
    o Things that aren't improvements will not be expanded

- Empower/enable people to make changes
  - o People have to be willing to change
  - o Need commitment to change
  - o Create a process for evaluating and making changes
- Have patience—be willing to put in the effort and wait for the payoffs

HOW TO APPLY AT YOUR COMPANY

If you're a regional distributor reading this, the key question becomes: How do I go about doing this at my company? Again, lean is not something you should take on alone; it's important to get outside help. However, as explained in chapter 5, there are some things that you can do to prepare for your lean journey. You can start the SBPI® process by gathering your executive team for an initiative start-up. Talk about the challenges your company is facing in the marketplace. Ask yourselves these general questions:

1. What is our mission?
2. What are our customers' needs?
3. What could we do to better anticipate those needs?
4. What are the key challenges in our marketplace today?
5. What do we want to accomplish in 5 years, 10 years?
6. How can we improve communication between our company and our suppliers, and customers?

Then ask yourselves these specific questions:

1. How do we add value?
2. What is value from the customer's perspective?
3. What are the transactions in our processes that the customer does not know or care for?
4. How many transactions do we have to commit to before we satisfy customers' requests?
5. What is our first-time pass?
6. Do we know our cost of processing orders?
7. What are the costs of errors in our system?
8. How do we lose customers?
9. How do we gain customers?
10. What is the cost of a lost customer?

11. What is the cost of carrying a customer?
12. What is our customer's point of entry into our system?
13. What are the regional characteristics of our customers?
14. What, if any, are our historical anchors for expansion?

As a regional distributor, you should choose a hub to focus on before going any further. The SBPI® process is done on a small scale basis first, not companywide. Once you've done that, identify the employees you would select for your cross-functional team to address the issues you've identified. Then bring that team together and further brainstorm some issues.

As with the national distributor example in chapter 5, once your team is in place, you can walk through the eight key steps of the SBPI® process:

1. Prioritize your list of issues, then select the top issues to be addressed. Develop a plan for gathering data on those issues.
2. Select the issue you'll tackle first--the issue for which you'll develop a PDSA (Plan-Do-Study-Act cycle, also described in chapter 4). Then plan your tests.
3. Brainstorm about how you would perform the tests, collect the data, and resolve any issues that may arise.
4. Discuss how you would analyze the data, what criteria you would use for accepting a change to an existing process, and how you would select a pilot.
5. Talk about how you would evaluate the pilot and how, if the pilot was successful, you would expand it into larger pilots.
6. Discuss the "dashboard" you would use to track the pilot; these are tools and measurements described in chapter 4. What information should you include in the dashboard? Also, decide who would be in your "quality circle"—the cross-functional team of employees charged with overseeing this particular process/system indefinitely.
7. Describe how you would test the proposed change(s) across the organization. Identify any risks and develop a plan to manage those risks.
8. Figure out how you would incorporate the change(s) in your company's regular operations. How would you communicate the change(s)—internally and externally to customers and suppliers?

CHAPTER 7

Real-World Example: Local Distributor

A particular local distributor (LD) has been in business for 8 years, with one distribution facility and two storefronts in a defined geographic area. This distributor has enjoyed extensive growth for the last few years and was planning for further growth in the local area. The distributor's management team recognized a need for structure in the operation to support growth and chose the SBPI$^®$ process as a structured approach to process design and implementation. After meeting with MCA, Inc.'s implementation team, the owner-operator president established his goals and objectives and started the lean initiative.

Exhibit 7-1 is a letter distributed from the LD CEO introducing the SBPI$^®$ process to his team. The steering committee consisted of the president, the CEO, and the CFO.

To: All employees

From: CEO

Re: Follow-up from last Thursday's Process Design Workshop

As we have made all of you aware previously, Local Distributor has contracted with MCA, Inc., to assist with the evaluation and recommendation of internal changes to help us grow in the coming years. As a result, many of you have seen MCA's team observing our work practices and methods over the past several weeks. Last Thursday, a group of managers and key individuals met to review these observations and to begin looking into how we as an organization should evaluate our activities and our ability to meet the needs of our customers during the planned growth phase.

As a result of this session, we formed three teams that will dig deeper into the way we operate, the cost of the way we operate, and the areas that we can best align ourselves to service the needs of our current and future customers. The three teams that have been formed are:

1. Sales

2. Production

3. Service.

Each team has been given a specific charter, which you may view in the attached files. The teams will meet weekly under the direction of an internal team leader and with the guidance of MCA. Throughout the months ahead, most employees will be asked to participate in supporting the efforts of these teams, through direct involvement on a team or through temporary brainstorming and idea evaluation, or through assistance with data collection.

We are proud of the level of commitment and involvement that each of our employees has expressed to date and we look forward to the input that each of you has to help LD become an even better company.

If you have any issues, concerns, or questions about this activity, please talk to me personally.

Thank you,
CEO
Local Distributor

Exhibit 7-1. Introduction Letter

The structure of the teams involved in the SBPI® process is shown in exhibit 7-2. The steering committee oversaw the sales, order processing, and service teams. The three teams were cross-functional, representing sales, sales support, warehouse positions, drivers, and accounting.

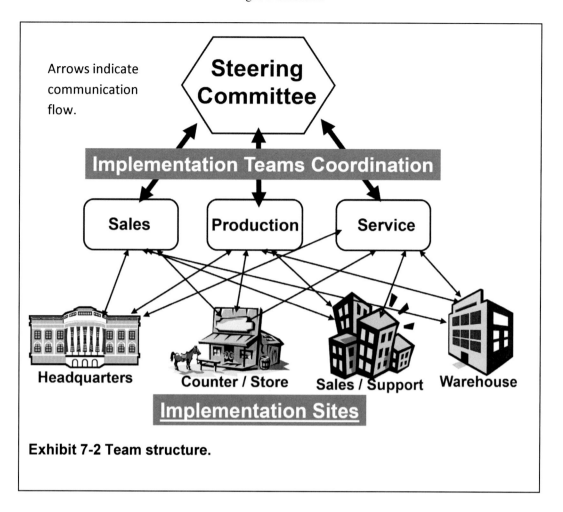

Exhibit 7-2 Team structure.

Each team developed a team charter to define its scope and to describe its overall objectives and timeline for achieving them. As an example, exhibit 7-3 shows the LD's sales team charter.

General Description:

Sales is a process that starts with the initial contact with the client and ends with assurance of accurate service and product delivery and customer satisfaction. It is a series of contacts, decisions, and actions that begin with the earliest steps of customer contact, estimation, quotation, and bidding and does not end until the job is purchased, including data and order entry into the system ready for ticket to be dropped at the warehouse. It is completed when improvement lessons are captured and integrated into standard methods of doing business.

Expected Results:

- Map the existing process of production, noting any exceptions that are driven by specific customer relationships
- Identify the potential activities that could be improved
- Suggest improvements and test on small scale
- Confirmed improvements will have the following characteristics:
  — Improve the process by better than 30%
  — Reduce the cost of operation by better than 5%
  — Are sustainable
  — Are trainable
  — Can be used across the company with minimal adjustments.

Make significant movement toward accomplishing objectives by end of year.

Exhibit 7-3. Local distributor: Sales team charter.

As with the examples in chapters 5 and 6, the local distributor's three teams started with an initial off-site meeting. Reviewing the overall company assessment, MCA Inc.'s implementation team introduced the SBPI® process. What follows is the flow of the lean implementation process through the application of SBPI®.

During the initial off-site meeting, the teams brainstormed areas of waste and rework in the entire LD operation. They identified cost drivers in the sales, order processing, and service areas. The following lists include some of those key issues:

Sales Cost Drivers

- Delay of order entry
- Not getting timely orders from the field (take time to ask; don't guess at what the customer is saying)
- Incomplete information
- Incorrect order entry
- Misinformation by customers
- Lack of timely order entry
- Time requests by customers
- Wrong item on order entry
- Miscommunication
- Not asking the right questions
- No communication or not enough communication regarding times and dates
- Lack of stock awareness
- Underutilized computer system
- Not placing direct orders on time--too much air freight

Production Cost Drivers

- Lack of specific procedures
- Lack of product knowledge
- Lack of training
- Improve fill rate
- Order pulling errors
- Not enough trucks (material being left behind)
- Pick tickets coming out late
- Will-call drivers returning late
- Material not stocked correctly (looking for material)
- Inadequate use of space
- Lack of communication
- Lack of training
- Receiving material—vendor or returns
- Loading of truck
- Pulling orders correctly—checking material

Service Cost Drivers

- Inaccurate information relating to will-call pickups
- Route planning
- Scheduling of deliveries
- Wrong addresses on ship tickets
- Communication with the foremen
- Redeliveries
- Late deliveries
- A will call that should have been direct shipped
- Emergency deliveries
- Staging and storage of material
- Kitting material
- Communication of material delivery times
- Same-day delivery
- Saturday deliveries
- Delivery management program/software

The team was then asked to rank the cost drivers according to their impact on the organization. The top five issues for each team to focus on are

Sales

1. Correct order entry
2. No communication or not enough communication regarding times and dates
3. Time requests by customers
4. Take time to ask—don't guess at what the customer is saying
5. Not placing direct orders on time—too much air freight

Production

1. Loading of truck
2. Inadequate use of space
3. Improve fill rate
4. Revamp the return process
5. Pulling orders correctly—checking material

<u>Service</u>

1. Redeliveries
2. Communication of material delivery times
3. Route planning
4. Delivery management software/program
5. Scheduling of deliveries

Process Mapping

After the initial session, the application of SBPI® started with the teams investigating the top issues. Flowcharting was used to establish the initial state of the current process and identify the data collection points throughout the process. Initially, due to lack of a visible structure within the local distributor's operation, the teams struggled to define process beginning and end points. Since their company is a local distributor, anyone in the operation is capable of performing any function. To the team members, the mind-set was: "do whatever it takes to get the material delivered to the customer." To start the data collection and process investigation, the team had to first identify the structure of the distributor's operations and which activities fell under each department or function (exhibit 7-4).

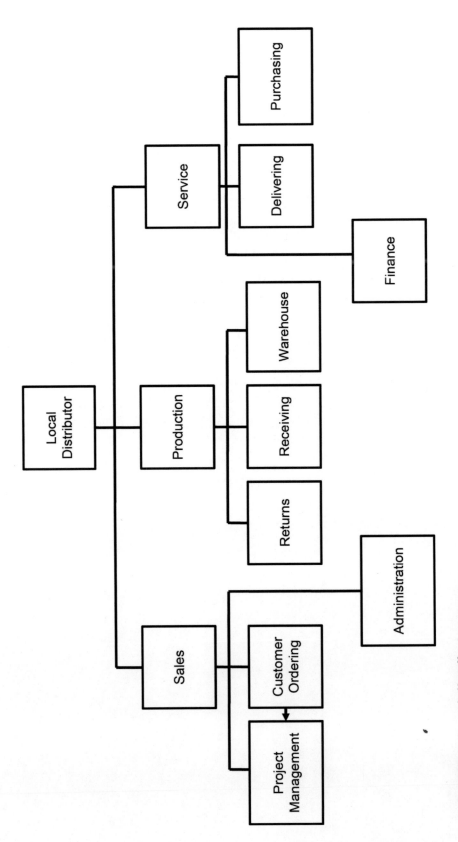

Exhibit 7-4. Local distributor process

Once those activities and their areas of application were clarified, teams were set up to develop flowcharts for project management, sales, order processing, delivery, and returns. LD's deployment flowchart for order processing is shown in exhibit 7-5.

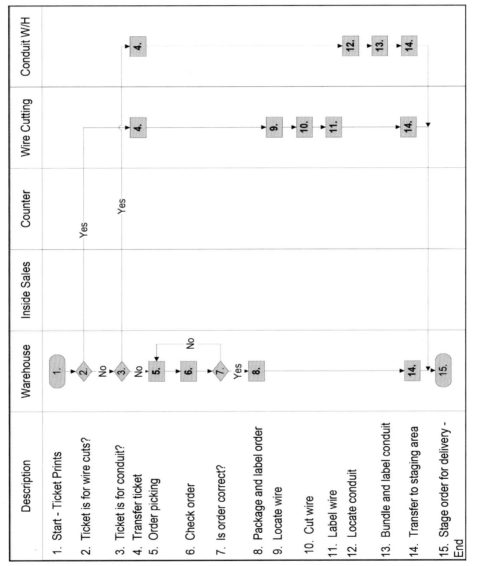

Exhibit 7-5. Deployment flowchart order processing.

Data Collection and Test Setup

Once the processes were made visible, the teams began to collect data to quantify the waste and rework in the system. One of the most important discoveries resulting from flowcharting was the fact that the system had more than expected lead time to pull orders. The time available to fill a third of the orders was more than 4 days. Additionally, it was established the 50% of the orders had less than 1 day of lead time. The importance of this discovery was more obvious when the segregation of the orders was changed from first-come first-serve to low-to-high lead time. The average of 3 minutes per line pulled was then used to improve the system throughput.

To establish baseline data for measuring improvements, the team measured its stock order to delivery cycle. The baseline data led the teams to develop PDSA tests in each area.

The sales team developed one PDSA focusing on the capacity for early time commitments for customers. A second PDSA was developed to change the cutoff time and the quantity allowed per day.

The service team focused on the returns process, with the goal of reducing the time to turn around credits on returned goods.

The order processing team developed a PDSA to reduce the pick time and increase the capacity in the warehouse. To investigate this PDSA, the team designed a test using a "master cell," which contained the 25 fastest-moving items in the warehouse in one location nearest the start and finish of the picking process. Exhibit 7-6 shows a Pareto chart the team used to identify the master cell items to move.

Running the Tests

The master cell PDSA resulted in increased capacity by 50% in the warehouse as shown in exhibit 7-7. This change was made by simply relocating products—no additional resources were added, meaning no costs were added to the process.

As a small company, the local distributor's structure enabled a much more nimble and quick application of the SBPI®. LD's design teams were able to test and validate PDSA cycles quickly, making changes and adjustments as needed. No formal approval processes or meetings were necessary to adopt the test results. As the master cell was developed, the process was refined through several short iterations of tests.

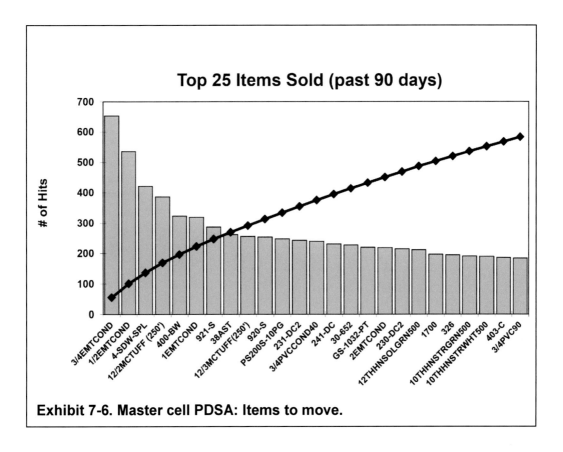

Exhibit 7-6. Master cell PDSA: Items to move.

Adoption of Proven Tests

The master cell PDSA was accepted and selected to become a concept to be expanded upon as a pilot. The order processing team reviewed the concept of the master cell and determined that locating product together according to the frequency of pulling was more effective than locating product together by manufacturer or product type. The pilot was designed to rearrange the entire warehouse into cell layout, with continuous flow of order production through the warehouse. The shelving was rearranged to allow items to be moved with one "sweep" of the shelves.

Stock Warehouse Process	Before	w/ Master Cell
Orders per day	270	
Ave. minutes to pull a line	2.1	1.6
Number of pullers	5	5
Max. line capacity for an 8 hr shift	1,000	1,500
Added capacity without added resources		50%
Assuming average line value	$130	
Gross Profit	20%	
Added Gross Profit per day		$10,000
Added Gross Profit per year		$2,640,000

Exhibit 7-7. Master cell overall impact.

Continuous Improvement

The pilot was successful, as measured by the same measures in the PDSA: faster pick times and fewer errors. The steering committee approved the pilot expansion, and the order processing team moved forward with additional process designs to improve warehouse capacity.

Product was laid out according to sales velocity, with fastest moving items closest to the start and end points of the cell and on eye-level shelves. Slow-moving items were "archived" in a secondary warehouse with the same setup.

Historically, the local distributor's pickers picked items in an order that was based on their experience and product knowledge. With the pilot expansion, the items were now printed on tickets in the order they would be pulled, allowing for much faster and consistent pick paths.

Due to the local distributor's smaller size, all the successful PDSAs evolved into full-size pilots and the last few steps of the SBPI® were therefore combined.

The local distributor's experience is applicable to regional and national distributors as well. The main issue remains the authority to proceed with the PDSAs as pilots at the local level. If national and regional distributors could allow local development of lean models, based on the nationally or regionally approved principles, they too could act efficiently in applying lean.

HOW TO APPLY AT YOUR COMPANY

If you're a local distributor, you can begin the SBPI® process the same way that national and regional distributors can: by gathering your executive team for an initiative start-up and brainstorming session. Talk about the challenges your company is facing in the marketplace, your long-term plans for growth, and what sets your company apart from the competition. Ask yourselves these general questions:

1. What is our company's mission?
2. What advantages do we have as a small company?
3. What disadvantages do we face?
4. What are our customers looking for?
5. How can we better serve our customers?
6. What are our long-term goals?

Then ask these specific questions:

1. How do we add value?
2. What is value from the customer's perspective?
3. What are the transactions in our processes that customers do not know or care for?
4. How many transactions do we have to commit to before we satisfy customers' requests?
5. What is our first-time pass?
6. Do we know our cost of processing orders?
7. What are the costs of errors in our system?
8. How do we lose customers?
9. How do we gain customers?
10. What is the cost of a lost customer?
11. What is the cost of carrying a customer?
12. What is our customer's point of entry into our system?

13. What, if any, are our historic anchors for expansion?
14. What is our niche market?
15. Why do we stay in business?
16. What is it we can offer that the national distributors can't?
17. How can we build on our strength as a local distributor?
18. Why do customers come to us?

If you have more than one branch, choose one where you will start the SBPI® process. Once you've done that, identify the employees you would select for your cross-functional team to address the issues you've identified. Then bring that team together and further brainstorm some issues.

As with the previous examples, once your team is in place, you can walk through the eight key steps of the SBPI® process:

2. Prioritize your list of issues then select the top issues to be addressed. Develop a plan for gathering data on those issues.
3. Select the issue you'll tackle first—the issue for which you'll develop a PDSA (Plan-Do-Study-Act cycle, also described in chapter 4). Then plan your tests.
4. Brainstorm about how you would perform the tests, collect the data and resolve any issues that may arise.
5. Discuss how you would analyze the data, what criteria you would use for accepting a change to an existing process, and how you would select a pilot.
6. Talk about how you would evaluate the pilot and how, if the pilot was successful, you would expand it into larger pilots.
7. Discuss the "dashboard" you would use to track the pilot; these are tools and measurements described in chapter 4. What information should you include in the dashboard? Also, decide who would be on your "quality circle" —the cross-functional team of employees charged with overseeing this particular process/system indefinitely.
8. Describe how you would test the proposed change(s) across the organization. Identify any risks and develop a plan to manage those risks.
9. Figure out how you would incorporate the change(s) in your company's regular operations. How would you communicate the change(s) —internally and externally to customers and suppliers?

CHAPTER 8

Survey Results

What is the status of lean in the wholesale distribution industry today? Do distributors understand lean concepts? Do they use lean concepts and principles to measure their performance and make improvements in their operations? And how does the wholesale distribution industry perform as a whole on key performance indicators? Could the wholesale distribution industry really benefit from implementing lean?

To answer these questions, a survey of NAW members was conducted specifically for this book. Members were asked about their familiarity with and use of some lean measurements discussed in the book, such as first-time pass, error tracking, and takt time. They were also asked for data on key industry performance measures, such as replenishment cycles and accounts receivable cycles. What follows are the survey results:

FIRST TIME PASS

The survey revealed that 41% of respondents indicated their company does not measure first time pass; another 23% said they do not know where or if first-time pass is tracked within their company. Of those companies that measure first-time pass, the majority measure it on an order-by-order basis (exhibit 8-1).

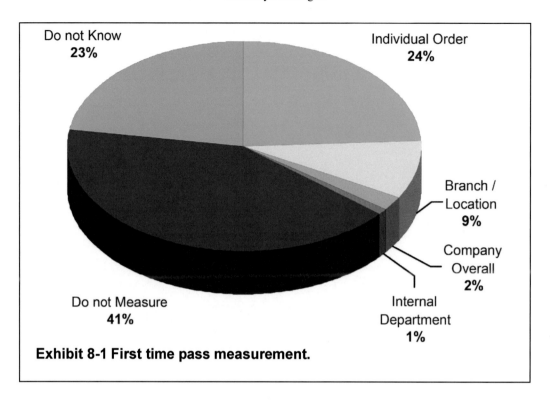

Do not Know
23%

Individual Order
24%

Branch /
Location
9%

Company
Overall
2%

Do not Measure
41%

Internal
Department
1%

Exhibit 8-1 First time pass measurement.

ERROR TRACKING

According to the survey, errors in the distribution process are tracked primarily in the warehouse. Sales, inventory management, service, and administration errors (such as billing and address errors) are tracked less frequently. Errors are more likely to be tracked if they occur in processes with tangible outputs (that is, orders in the warehouse), as well as in processes that occur in a single physical area (exhibit 8-2).

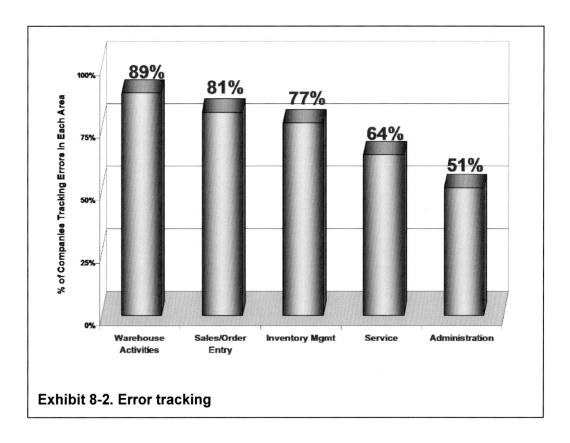

Exhibit 8-2. Error tracking

TAKT TIME

Only 11% of companies indicated that they measure takt time—the average system time between customer cycles. Of those, the majority of the "yes" respondents are locally managed companies or branches. Less than 2% of the respondents measure takt time at a corporate level (exhibit 8-2).

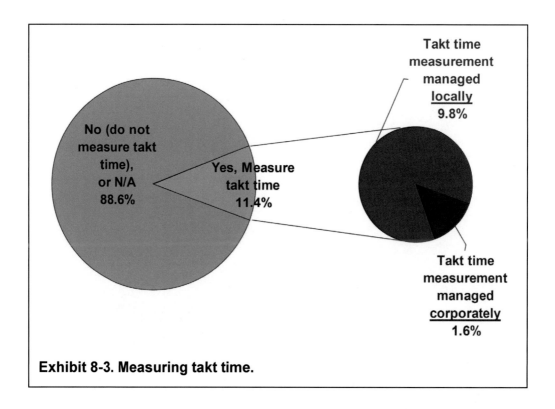

Exhibit 8-3. Measuring takt time.

FILLING ORDERS UPON RECEIPT OF ORDER

Less than half (44%) of companies indicated that they are able to fill more than 95% of orders at receipt of the order. Almost a quarter, (24%) indicated that more than 10% of orders cannot be immediately filled (exhibit 8-4).

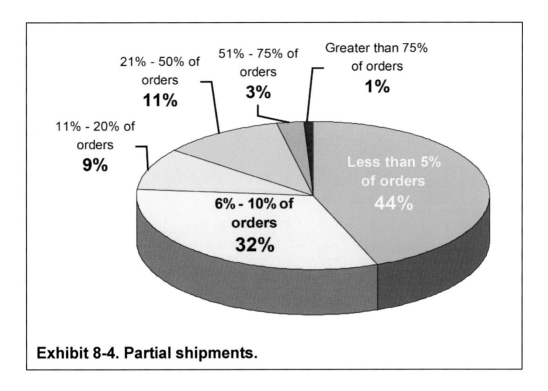

21% - 50% of orders
11%

51% - 75% of orders
3%

Greater than 75% of orders
1%

11% - 20% of orders
9%

Less than 5% of orders
44%

6% - 10% of orders
32%

Exhibit 8-4. Partial shipments.

SMALL COMPANY SHIPMENTS

Small customers (those with less than $50,000 in orders) are most impacted by delayed or incomplete orders. In fact, 75% of respondents said that they are unable to completely fill at least 90% of orders for their small customers. Large customers' orders are filled completely every time, based on the survey response (exhibit 8-5).

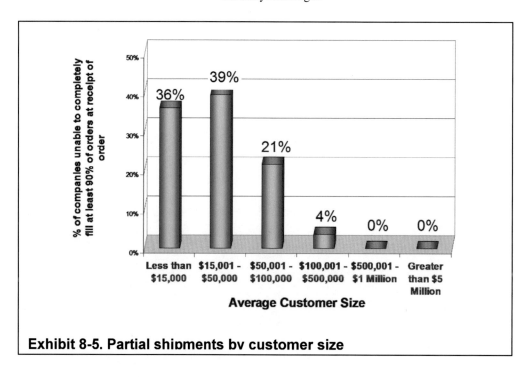

Exhibit 8-5. Partial shipments by customer size

REPLENISHMENT CYCLE

The replenishment cycle for wholesaler-distributors is more than 3 weeks for typical stock-keeping units (SKU). In other words, most distributors carry more than 3 weeks of inventory for the items sold most often (exhibit 8-6).

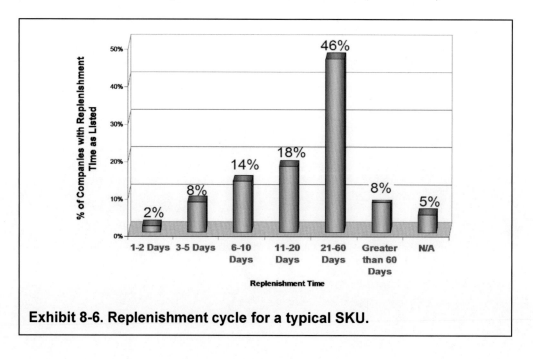

Exhibit 8-6. Replenishment cycle for a typical SKU.

About 50% of companies, regardless of the number of SKUs they carry, replenish/reorder their own inventory every 3 to 8 weeks (21 to 60 days). Larger companies (those with more than 60,000 SKUs) have a smaller range of replenishment time. Almost all of their SKUs are replenished within 1 to 8 weeks. Smaller companies may replenish SKUs anywhere between 1 day and more than 2 months (exhibit 8-7).

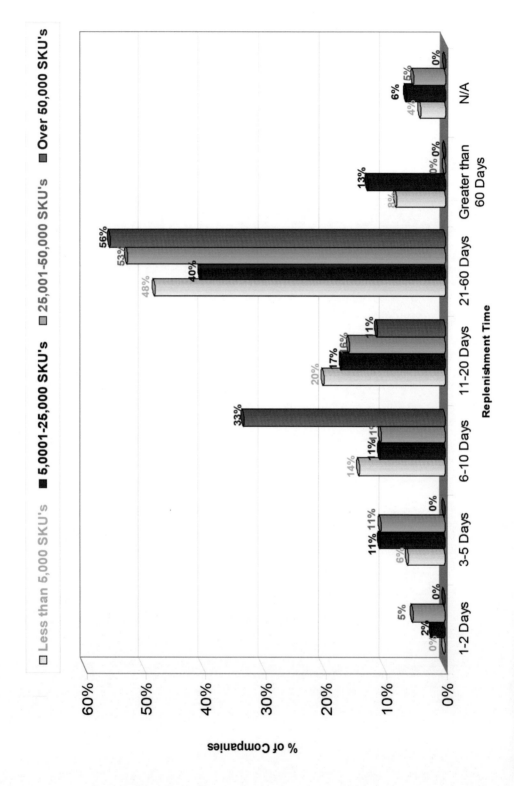

Exhibit 8-7. Replenishment Cycle for all SKUs.

EXPEDITING ORDERS

In this area, 39% of respondents indicated that at least 10% of their orders receive some form of expediting during the process; 12% responded that more than 25% receive expediting; and 5% responded that more than 50% receive expediting. Although the largest category shows that few orders require expediting, more than one in every three orders needs time and effort spent on expediting (exhibit 8-8).

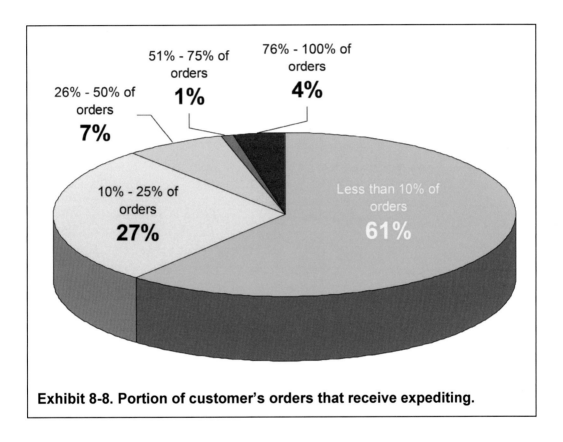

Exhibit 8-8. Portion of customer's orders that receive expediting.

RESOURCES NEEDED FOR ORDER DELIVERY

Most companies indicated that more than 15% of sales revenue is required to handle or process the delivery to the customer. This means that the cost to get the order from the warehouse to the customer eats away at 15% of the sales dollars that the order brought in (exhibit 8-9).

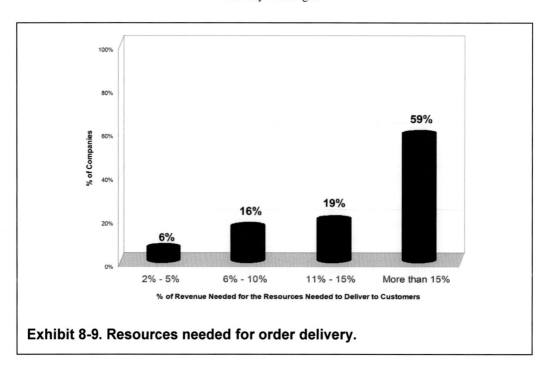

Exhibit 8-9. Resources needed for order delivery.

RETURNS

Only 12% of companies reprocess more than 5% of their sales as returns. Of those companies, small companies (those with less than $100 million in revenue) represent the majority at 9%. Large companies' returns typically do not make up more than 5% of their annual revenue (exhibit 8-10).

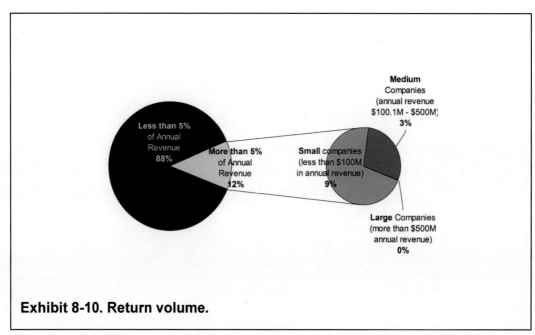

Exhibit 8-10. Return volume.

ACCOUNTS RECEIVABLE COLLECTION CYCLE

The survey revealed that 43% of respondents indicated that it takes more than 41 days to receive payment for sales. The vast majority of companies (96%) operate with typical payment cycles more than 21 days. Only 4% have payment within 20 days (exhibit 8-11).

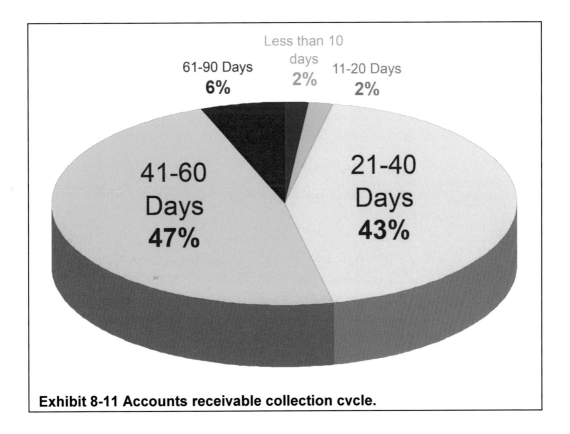

Exhibit 8-11 Accounts receivable collection cvcle.

SMALL COMPANY CASH FLOW

Small companies are far more likely to operate without the cash flow from collected receivables. Small companies (those with less than $100 million in annual revenue) have more than 10% of their accounts receivable older than 60 days, whereas larger companies have none. Small companies have no outstanding receivables younger than 20 days, whereas 2% of medium companies' receivable and 20% of large companies' receivable are less than 20 days old (exhibit 8-12).

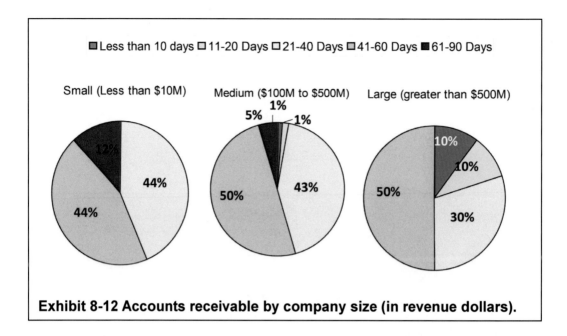

Exhibit 8-12 Accounts receivable by company size (in revenue dollars).

These survey results reveal much about the wholesale distribution industry. The data show that most distributors do not track key lean measurements, such as first-time pass and takt time, and that their error measurements are concentrated in the warehouse, with little attention paid to other departments, such as sales and administration. The data also show that distributors, on the whole, could stand to make substantial improvements on key performance measures, such as order fill rates, replenishment cycles, and accounts receivable cycles.

In essence, wholesaler-distributors can benefit greatly by implementing lean concepts. Lean thinking means taking a big-picture view of your company's operations, analyzing your processes and procedures, then taking steps to make them more streamlined and efficient—always keeping customer service in the forefront.

A FINAL WORD

The theories, tools, and examples introduced in this book serve as guidelines for wholesaler-distributors that want to become lean. In a lean distributorship, waste is minimized throughout the organization; every order is produced at the lowest possible cost and meets all customer expectations of time, cost, and quality. Improving a distributor's throughput, however, can't be achieved by pursuing lean in just one or another part of the company. The entire distributorship must pursue lean and become more productive overall in order for lean benefits to translate into profits. And just like any athlete, a lean wholesaler-distributor needs constant and consistent opportunity to practice, exercise, and improve. Again, lean is about continuous improvement.

The sole purpose of pursuing lean should be to increase profits through higher customer satisfaction. In an industry such as wholesale distribution, these profitability gains come when the distributor is a low-cost producer of orders and service. It is impossible to be a low-cost producer without being lean. And to become lean, the distributorship must be designed with its customers' needs as the main focus point.

Perhaps most importantly, lean starts with your company's top managers. Although the details of implementing and applying lean must be carried out by everyone in the company—at all levels of the company—the ultimate responsibility for lean cannot be passed on or delegated; it must be held, discussed, and practiced by top management, whose responsibility is to foster an operational philosophy and culture that embraces lean in all aspects of the business.

Lean is not a destination, it is a journey.

APPENDIX A

Organizational Learning, Methods and Tools

ORGANIZATIONAL LEARNING

In today's environment of quickly changing markets, learning and adaptation are as critical to companies as their daily operations and income. Organizations without continuous learning and continuous improvement processes designed to be part of their daily activities cannot achieve or maintain leadership positions in their field.

For example, there are three levels of organizational learning, (Argyris, 1993):

- **Primary Organizational Learning:** Finding solutions to immediate individual issues.
- **Secondary Organizational Learning**: The improvement of procedures and methods.
- **Tertiary Organizational Learning:** The development of changes in processes, principles and/or operational models.

These levels can be illustrated by examining a conflict, such as the discrepancy between inventory as measured by an inventory tracking system and inventory as measured by a physical count (exhibit A-1).

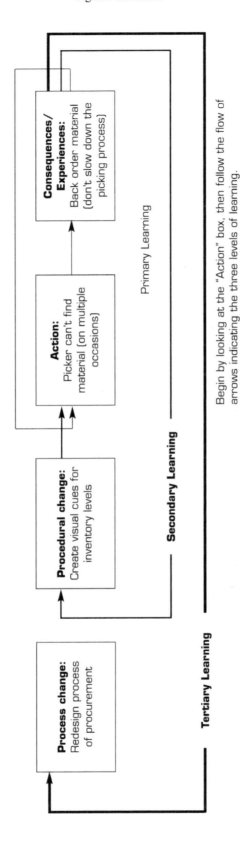

Exhibit A-1 Learning Levels

Primary Organizational Learning

Primary learning addresses immediate issues by using conflict-resolution methods. For example, a picker may go to the shelf and note that an item is not available even though the inventory system indicates two available—in this case, physical count indicates zero. At the primary level, this particular picker may learn that the material is on another shelf, in a secondary location, received but not put away, miscounted, and so on. He will solve the problem by either finding the material, which would add unnecessary work to his own process, or entering a back order, which would add unnecessary work to the system.

Secondary Organizational Learning

Secondary learning is triggered to improve the procedures and streamline a portion of the process. For example, if this item is regularly not available when the system shows that it is, a procedural improvement might be implemented, such as a red-tag system that automatically indicates the physical inventory level or an automatic cue to a secondary location if the first is empty. These are process-based improvements that are based on individual occurrences, which showed that either the buffers were too small for the daily turns or the material was often stored in a secondary location. These improvements eliminated the need for individual response to an empty location.

Tertiary Organizational Learning

Tertiary learning occurs at the company level when the results from secondary learning improvements indicate that an entire process must be redesigned. If, for instance, the discrepancy occurs in this example because the receiving process allows material to be available in the system before it is available on the shelf, the entire receiving process—or possibly the entire procurement process—may need to be redesigned.

Corporate Memory

Another component to organizational learning is corporate memory, which is the total body of data, information, and knowledge required to deliver a company's strategic aims and objectives. As wholesaler-distributors grow, the company leader cannot be everywhere at once and cannot serve as a singular point for all company knowledge. The distributor must define and standardize its processes and procedures so that all employees can adequately complete their jobs. By including more departments in more processes, and capitalizing on cross-functional knowledge, distributors emphasize structured communication flow as well as a wide communication bandwidth, which is a tenet of the lean operational model. The feedback loop and corporate memory need to be developed system wide to include customers and suppliers. Exhibit A-2 shows the issues and functions that should be part of a company's corporate memory; the arrows indicate the communication flow between the customer and the distributor's various departments and how that communication, in turn, contributes to corporate memory.

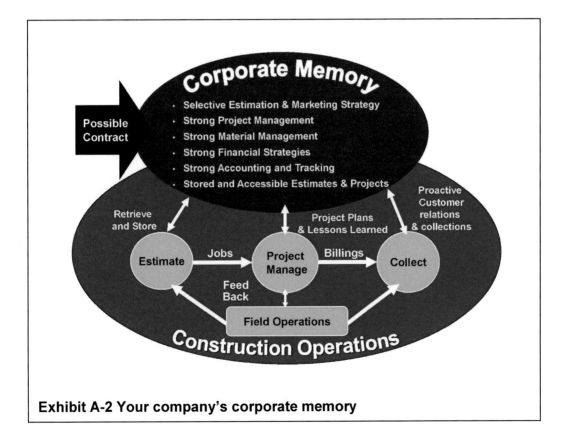

Exhibit A-2 Your company's corporate memory

METHODS AND TOOLS

Aspirations of quick results, in conjunction with a lack of strategic thinking, have forced many companies to look for "silver bullets" in tools and technologies (Farrell, 2003). The reality stands in sharp contrast: The application of information technology alone does not improve productivity. Using technological tools without a definite strategy will, in the best case, keep a company at par with its current productivity levels. The lean principles of the Toyota Production System go so far as to state that "Any system [that] has a series of new technologies growing faster than the capacity to detect problems will invariably fail" (Yoshimura, 2002).

Tools are not the silver bullet. When you buy IT solutions, you are purchasing more than just an application—you are also buying the business model as developed and promoted by the programmer. For example, every Enterprise Resource Planning (ERP) system has an underlying business model in which it makes sense to operate. If a company doesn't agree with the entire business model as delivered with the ERP program, they must internally change the programming or discard portions of the system, either of which may bear prohibitive cost.

Well defined change management processes can offer huge benefits in promoting a lean culture when they are correctly supported by appropriately used technology. However, the process must drive the selection: The use of the tool must follow the process and not the other way around. Technology tools need to focus on the correct aspects of the system: They must promote visibility and visible measurements of the system, accelerate organizational learning, and promote the development of a corporate memory. A lean distributor must design its processes prior to committing to program or IT solutions.

Any methodology for improvement must also be process based and remain focused on the entire system. Strategic Breakthrough Process Improvement (SBPI®), described in chapter 4, is the process for transforming an entire wholesale distribution company into an efficient, cost-effective delivery system for products and services. The SBPI® process provides a structure for identifying areas that need improvement, implementing appropriate improvements, and continuously monitoring the system for ongoing improvement. Process maps, Plan-Do-Study-Act (PDSA) cycles, issue resolution, project management, and system measures such as Customer Positioning and Control (CPAC®) are among the tools that support the SBPI® process. See chapter 4 for more information.

APPENDIX B

Calculating First-Time Pass Yield

First-Time Pass, also called system yield, measures the rate of error-free production of orders and services. It also measures the errors that occur at each step in a process or procedure. A lean process occurs when first-time pass yield is nearing 100%: rework and non-essential steps have been eliminated and capacity is efficiently utilized.

Use equations discussed below to calculate first-time pass yield. To start, here are some definitions:

S = number of orders entering production

P = number of orders produced on first-time pass

PX = number of orders produced on first-time pass at step X

E = number of orders that have errors

EX = number of orders that have errors at step X. These errors are fixed at the same step where they occurred.

EXY = number of orders that have errors at step X and must be returned to step Y.

Exhibit B-1 shows the three-step order production process (simplified to sales, warehouse, and delivery) and possible rework loops.

The number of orders entering the system (S) and the number of errors at each step in the process (E) are measured values, all of which can be tracked. The number of error-free line items (P) for each step is calculated by subtracting E from S. To calculate the first-time pass yield for step one, use the following equation with 1 indicating that these steps occur in step one: $\mathbf{P1 = S - E1}$.

When calculating the first-time pass yield of a system, a wholesaler-distributor must consider the first-time pass yield of each step. The error-free order from the sales procedures in step one (P1) should be used as the input for step two (warehouse). The first-time pass yield for step two (P2) is the number of sales orders (P1) entering the warehouse, minus the errors (E2) made and discovered in the warehouse, and minus the errors that were made in sales and not discovered until they reached the warehouse (E21): $\mathbf{P2 = P1 - E2 - E21}$.

The same method is used to calculate the first-time pass yield of the remaining steps in the process. The total first-time pass yield of the system (PX) is the sum of the first-time pass yield of each step. In this equation, X represents the number of steps in your order process (or any process): $P_X = P_{x-1} - E_x - E_{x\,(x-1)} - E_{x\,(x-2)} - E_{x2} - E_{x1}$

Ultimately, in this equation, P_X represents the percentage of error-free orders delivered to the customer.

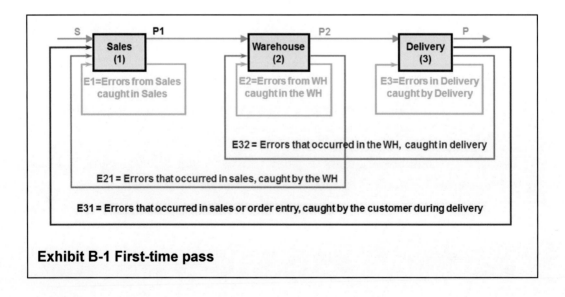

Exhibit B-1 First-time pass

APPENDIX C

Plan-Do-Study-Act (PDSA) Cycles

The PDSA process provides a structure for learning while a potential change is tested. A process in which there is opportunity for improvement often presents many potential opportunities. The PDSA process raises questions such as: What are we trying to accomplish? How will we know that a change is an improvement? What changes can we make that will result in improvement?

Many organizations pursue solutions by instituting a change and hoping it works. Every improvement comes from a change, but not every change is an improvement. From the list of issues the distributor identifies for improvement, a list of potential PDSA cycles can be derived. PDSA cycles should be short in duration. A small change is tested, adjustments are made, and it is tested again. The PDSA suggestions may come from suggestions on what to change.

Part of the selection process also includes identifying the scope of the PDSA and the functions within the organization that "touch" the process being studied. Use the following sets of questions and directives to help develop each stage of the PDSA cycle:

Plan:

Define the System

1. Which company standard/procedure is being addressed? Why?
2. What improvements in the system are being looked for?
3. How is the organization currently planning for improvements?
4. How is the current planning impacting the organizational learning?
5. What data should be collected to measure the current method of planning and its impact on the organization?

Assess the Current Situation

1. What is known about the organization's current level of learning?
2. How is the organization currently performing?
3. Collect baseline data according to the measures selected in "Define the System."

Analyze the Cause

1. What could be the cause of the organizational results that currently are achieved?
2. Can the root cause that is producing the current results be identified?
3. Develop a theory: What planning strategies will improve organizational output and learning?

Do:

Try Out the Improvement Theory

1. Develop an action plan based on the root causes identified and the improvement theory created in the previous steps.
2. Determine the necessary steps to carry out the action.
3. Collect data again after several weeks of implementing the test plan and compare to the baseline data.

Study:

Study the Results

1. Did the improvement theory work? What improvements in the organizational throughput and learning have occurred?
2. What changes have occurred in planning for improvements?

Standardize Improvement

1. How has the organization's planning for improvement changed?
2. Will the changes be sustainable?

3. Has the organization's ability to learn improved as a result of planning for improvement/change?
4. How will the future impact of change planning be measured on organizational learning?

Act:

Plan for Continuous Improvement

1. Accept or reject the change.
2. If the test is successful, how will the pilot be planned?
3. What is the next area of the organization in which to use the PDSA cycle?

PLAN TESTS

Every PDSA cycle starts with an assumption. Assumptions are not necessarily true, but they are used as the basis for the systems and processes—*as if they were true.* Assumptions form a theory; a theory is an integrated set of principles that explain and predict observed events.

During the planning stage of the PDSA cycle, the goals, test objectives, and objectives of the change are clearly stated. Measurements and details are outlined, as are the expected results and an anticipated next learning cycle:

- Description of change to be tested (who, what, when, how long)
- Expected results (counts, observations, measurements)
- Measurement of the results
- Method for analyzing results
- Plan for the next PDSA cycle: What is the learning objective? What does the company want to learn from the PDSA cycle?

The success of any PDSA cycle hinges on the answers to these questions. Without a clear understanding of the reason for testing and a solid plan for how to evaluate the outcome, it is difficult to measure the success of the test. Exhibit C-1 is an example of a form wholesaler-distributors can use to capture the PDSA assumptions and applications.

The results of the test do not always match the expectations, however. During the test, the productivity may worsen, but that does not mean it is time to abandon the test.

PDSA FORM
(for Testing an Change Aimed at Improvement)

Overall Project Name:

PDSA Name:

PDSA # or line item # from project plan:

QC / Design Team Leader:

PDSA Leader:

What is the overall work of the project trying to accomplish?

What is the purpose of <u>this</u> PDSA Cycle—what do you intend to learn?

How will you know that a change is an improvement?

PLAN — Plan a change/test aimed at improvement. Details of the plan:

- Describe the change to be tested (who, what, when—how long, where, how, etc.).

  ➢

- Describe the results you expect to produce. Answer in this form: **If we do this** ___ (specific action), **then we will get this result** ___ (specific results in units of measure, counts, observations, answers to questions, etc.)

  ➢

- How will the results be measured?

  ➢

- What will the next PDSA cycle be designed to learn?

  ➢

DO — Perform the test. Collect data.

- Was the test performed as planned? Explain.
  - ➢ [   ]

- Describe how the test went.
  - ➢ [   ]

- What data and observations were created during the test (attach documentation)?
  - ➢ [   ]

STUDY — Compare what happened to what you expected to happen. Answer the question: "Now, what do you know".

- Were the results of the test studied as planned? Explain
  - ➢ [   ]

- Results of analysis (attach findings):
  - ➢ [   ]

- Describe how the test worked? Compare your predictions to the test results.
  - ➢ [   ]

- Is the change an improvement? Describe (Attach any supporting documentation, such as control charts).
  - ➢ [   ]

ACT — Decide: Adopt, abandon, or re-test the change.
- Describe the next steps and planned PDSA cycles
  - ➢ [   ]

- Are the next planned actions rational based on what was learned from your test? Explain.
  - ➢ [   ]

Exhibit C-1 PDSA Form

PERFORM TESTS

Once the test has been planned and the baseline measurements are in place, the next step is to perform the test as planned. Clear instructions may be needed if the testers have not been involved in the PDSA selection and plan until this point.

COLLECT DATA

Data are reported throughout the PDSA test step. It is critical to report on findings and lessons learned, since the PDSA cycle is a structure for learning. While the test is in progress, the organization may learn something entirely new about the system. This new knowledge may prompt another PDSA cycle or an alteration to the plan.

The data collection should be as consistent and thorough as possible. If the data collection is abandoned at any point in the test, the group will end up lacking the information needed to make a decision about the PDSA cycle.

There are various types of data. Categorical data exist when data are grouped by certain characteristics—for example, all items shipped by trucks or all items picked twice, and so forth Counts, or frequencies, are collected when counting the number of instances (that is, number of back orders) —the count can be a pure count or a proportion of a population (a sample). Rankings and ratings give comparison data within a list. Variable data are used for quantitative measures for a particular scale—for example, activity times, first-time pass, and so on. The types of data gathered will require the selection of the appropriate measures and tools for analysis.

There are also rules for presenting data:

Rule 1: Data should always be presented in such a way that preserves the evidence in the data for all the predictions that might be made from it.

- A table of values should accompany most graphs, and context for the data should be completely and fully described:
  - Who collected the data?
  - How were the data collected?
  - What do these values represent?
  - If the data are computed values, how were the values computed from the raw inputs?

Rule 2: Whenever an average, range, or histogram (bar chart) is used to summarize data, the summary should not mislead the user into taking any action that he would not take if the data were presented in *time series* (as in a run chart).

- o Averages, ranges, and histograms all obscure the time order of the data.
- o If the time order of the data shows some sort of definite pattern, then the obscuring of this pattern by the use of averages, ranges, or histograms can mislead the user.
- o Since all data occur in time, virtually all data will have a time order.
- o In some cases, this time order is the essential context that must be preserved in the presentation.

For more information and further study of PDSA cycles, consult the work of Walter A. Shewhart, listed in the References and Resources section.

GLOSSARY

Capacity, Capability, and Throughput

The capacity of your system is measured by the maximum production (the number of orders, lines, deliveries, and so on) that can be processed through the system at peak efficiency. The capability measures how many orders can be processed with current operational practices and efficiencies. And throughput is measured by how much input material has been converted into sales.

Corporate Memory (CM)

CM includes established processes and procedures to improve the value delivery system and to learn continuously from internal mistakes or external influence factors. CM can be defined as the total body of data, information, and knowledge required to deliver the strategic aims and objectives of an organization. CM is not unlike the human brain—as it gains more experience it improves its knowledge. CM is the memory in an organization that enables translation of data to information to knowledge to wisdom. The people who interact with those data will be able to learn, make decisions, understand context, or find colleagues with the same level of understanding.

CM can be subdivided into the following types:

- Professional (reference material, documentation, tools, methodologies)
- Company (organizational structure, activities, products, participants)
- Individual (status, competencies, know-how, activities)
- Project (definition, activities, histories, results)

When exploring CM, these key questions must be answered:

- What knowledge representation should be used (for example, stories, patterns, cases, rules, predicate logic, and so on)?

- Who will the users be? What are their information and learning needs?
- How should security be ensured and who will be granted access?
- How should CM best be integrated with existing sources, stores, and
systems?

- What should be done to ensure that the current content is correct, applicable, timely, and weighted?
- How should experts be motivated to contribute?
- What should be done about ephemeral insights, and how should informal scripts (for example, e-mail and instant messenger posts) be captured?

Alternative and related terms are organizational memory, group memory, knowledge base, and knowledge repository.

Customer Positioning and Control (CPAC®)

CPAC® is a measurement process and tool used for verification of improvements through various initiatives. CPAC® uses a four-quadrant positioning method to evaluate a customer or operation based on recognized profits and revenues. The components of the operation are divided into cost codes according to the type of work. The cost codes are positioned according to their draw on the effort (labor hours) and cost needed to address each specific end user's demands on the distributor's resources.

Cycle Time

Cycle time is the total elapsed time to move an order from the beginning to the end of a process, as defined by a distributor's activities and by the customer. Cycle time includes process time, during which an order is acted upon to bring it closer to delivery, and delay time, during which the order is waiting to take the next action.

First-Time Pass

First-Time Pass, also called system yield, measures the rate of error-free production of goods and services. It also measures the errors that occur at each step in a process or procedure. A lean process occurs when first-time pass yield is nearing 100%: rework and non-essential steps have been eliminated and capacity is efficiently utilized.

Game Theory

Game Theory describes the customer's perspective on the products and services he receives: "The customer will judge value of a service (perceived quality) based on the utilities received in exchange for capital and effort," (Nash, 1996). The reverse is also true; a distributor's profitable customers are those that use the least amount of capital and effort (resources) for the services or products provided.

Hawthorne Effect

This occurs when people involved in a research study temporarily change their behavior or performance as a result of the observation rather than the actual test. The effect is named for the Hawthorne Works—a large factory complex in Illinois that operated from 1905 to 1983—where one study in a series of experiments on factory workers investigated the effect of lighting on workers' productivity. Researchers found that productivity almost always increased after a change in illumination, no matter what the level of illumination was--leading to the conclusion that it was the experience of being in a test that affected the results.

Kaizen

Kaizen is a Japanese word for "change for the better" or "improvement"; the common English usage is "continual improvement."

Kaizen is a daily activity whose purpose goes beyond simple productivity improvement. It is also a process that, when done correctly, humanizes the workplace and eliminates overly hard work (both mental and physical). It teaches people how to perform experiments on their work using the scientific method and how to learn to spot and eliminate waste in business processes.

Kaizen Event

In the United States, kaizen is often synonymous with "kaizen blitz" or "kaizen event." Such events rapidly implement work cells, improve setups, or streamline processes. However, a better Japanese word for this activity is *kaikaku*.

Little's Law

Little's Law states: The average number of orders in a queuing system Work in Process (WIP) is equal to the average Output Rate (OR) of orders from that system, times the average time spent in that system—System Cycle Time (SCT). The Little's Law equation looks like this: SCT = WIP x OR.

Plan-Do-Study-Act (PDSA) Cycles

The PDSA process provides a structure for learning while a potential change is tested. A process in which there is opportunity for improvement often presents many potential opportunities.

Dr. W.E. Deming called it the Shewhart cycle (Shewhart, 1923), giving credit to its inventor, Dr. Walter A. Shewhart. The Japanese have always called it the Deming cycle in honor of the contributions Deming made to Japan's quality improvement efforts over many years. Some people simply call it the PDCA— Plan, Do, *Check,* Act cycle. Regardless of its name, the idea is well-known to process improvement engineers, quality professionals, quality improvement teams, and others involved in continuous improvement efforts. The model can be used for the ongoing improvement of almost anything and it contains the following four continuous steps: Plan, Do, Study, and Act.

Process of Production

Production in distribution includes all the activities required to:

    a. Take an order
    b. Process the order through sales
    c. Process the order throughout warehouse by:
        i. Looking for items
        ii. Picking items
            1. Reporting back orders
            2. Reporting pick exceptions
            3. Reporting damages
            4. Reporting misplaced items
        iii. Packing
        iv. Inspecting
            1. Reporting shortages

          2. Reporting wrong picks
- v. Shipping
    1. Routing optimization
    2. Reporting wrong addresses
    3. Managing returns
- vi. Returns
    1. Receiving
    2. Restocking
    3. Reporting for credit
- vii. Receiving
    1. Receiving physical inventory
    2. Receiving e-inventory
    3. Stocking
    4. Filing shortage report
    5. Filing damage report
    6. Insurance claims

Standard Work

Standard work defines the most efficient methods to produce product using available equipment, people, and material. Standard work depicts the key process points, operator procedures, production sequence, safety issues, and quality checks. It must identify the amount and location of WIP inventory in the cell. Developing standard work is one of the more difficult lean disciplines. Once you start to implement flow and pull systems, your workers can get caught up in the dynamic changes and behind in documenting those changes.

Statistical Process Control (SPC)

SPC is a methodology developed by both Drs. Shewhart and Deming for monitoring a process through the use of control charts. It is a tool used to measure the process variation from its nominal goal. SPC relies on collection of data from samples at various points within the process. With SPC, variations in the process that may affect the quality of the end product or service can be detected and corrected, thus reducing waste as well as the likelihood that problems will be passed on to the customer. SPC emphasizes early detection and prevention of problems. SPC has a distinct advantage over quality methods, such as inspection, that apply resources to detecting and correcting problems in the end product or service.

In addition to reducing waste, SPC can lead to a reduction in the time required to produce the product or service from end to end. This is partially due to a diminished likelihood that the final product will have to be reworked, but it may also result from using SPC data to identify bottlenecks, wait times, and other sources of delays within the process. Process cycle time reductions, coupled with improvements in yield, have made SPC a valuable tool from both a cost reduction and a customer satisfaction standpoint.

Strategic Breakthrough Process Improvement (SBPI®)

SBPI® enables a wholesaler-distributor to apply the principles of lean operations in manageable sections without losing sight of the overall transformation. SBPI® is the step-by-step guide for application of lean principles.

Takt Time

Takt time, derived from the German word *taktzeit* (beat time) and translated as "clock cycle," is the maximum time allowed to produce a product in order to meet demand. In a lean company, the pace of production flow will be determined to best respond to this takt time or demand cycle time. The product flow cycle should be no longer than the takt time. Takt time is a theoretical calculation, calculated by dividing the available production time by the rate of customer demand (output demand).

Value Stream Mapping

Value stream mapping is a lean technique used to analyze the flow of materials and information currently required to bring a product or service to a consumer. At Toyota, where the technique originated, it is known as "material and information flow mapping."

REFERENCES AND RESOURCES

REFERENCES

Argyris, Chris. (1993). *On Organizational Learning*. Cambridge, MA: Blackwell Publishers.

Daneshgari, Dr. Parviz (Perry). (1998). *The Chase*. San Diego, CA: Black Forest Press.

Farrell, Diana. (October 2003). "The *Real* New Economy." Boston, MA: *Harvard Business Review*.

GM PowerTrain. (1991). *Methods for Continual Improvement.* Pontiac, MI. General Motors Corporation.

Joiner, Brian. (1994). <u>*Fourth Generation Management.*</u> New York: McGraw-Hill, Inc.

Moen, Ronald, Thomas W. Nolan, and Lloyd P. Provost. (1991). *Improving Quality Through Planned Experimentation*. New York: McGraw-Hill, Inc.

Nash, John. (1996). *Essays on Game Theory*. Williston, VT: Edward Elgar Publishing Inc.

Shewhart, W.A., Ph.D. (1923). *Economic Control of Quality of Manufactured Product.* Chelsea, MI.: ASQ Quality Press.

Swartz, James. (1994). *The Hunters and the Hunted*. Portland, OR: Productivity Press.

Taylor, Fredick. (1911). *Principles of Scientific Management.* New York & London: Harper & Brothers Publishers.

Yoshimura, Tatsuhiko (2002). *Mizenboushi Metho.* Tokyo, Japan: JUSE Press Ltd.

RESOURCES

Brigham, Eugene F. (1989). *Fundamentals of Financial Management, 5th edition.* Orlando, FL: The Dryden Press, a division of Holt, Rinehart, and Winston, Inc.

Daneshgari, Dr. Parviz (Perry) and Gene Dennis. (1998). "Inventory Management Through Supplier Partnership." National Electrical Contractors Association, Presentation. Las Vegas, NV.

Daneshgari, Dr. Parviz (Perry), Mike Romanowski, and Thomas Stimson. (1996). "Application of QFD Correlation Matrix Technology to Engine Development Time." Warrendale, PA: Society of Automotive Engineers.

Daneshgari, Dr. Parviz (Perry) and S.J. Harbin. (2003). *Procurement Chain Management in the Construction Industry,* Bethesda, MD: The Electrical Contracting Foundation, Inc.

Heragu, Sunderesh. (1997). *Facilities Design.* Boston, MA: PWS Publishing Company.

Kotabe, M., Martin, X. and Domoto, H. (2003, April). Gaining from Vertical Partnerships: Knowledge Transfer Relationship Duration and Supplier Performance Improvement in the U.S. and Japanese Automotive Industries. *Strategic Management Journal* Vol. *24*(4): 293.

Mayer Electric Supply Company's Lean Documentation. (2006).

McCormack, Kevin P., William C. Johnson, and William T. Walker. (2003). *Supply Chain Networks & Business Process Orientation, Advanced Strategies and Best Practices.* Boca Raton, FL: CRC Press LLC.

Rigsbee, Ed. (2000) *Partner Shift.* New York: John Wiley & Sons Inc.

Schechter, Damon, and Gordon Sander. (2002). *Delivering the Goods.* Hoboken, NJ: John Wiley & Sons, Inc.

Tompkins, James A., John A.White, Yavuz A. Bozer, Edward H. Frazelle, J.M.

A. Tanchoco, and Jaime Trevino. (1996). *Facilities Planning, 2nd edition.* Toronto, Ontario, Canada: John Wiley & Sons Canada, Ltd.

ABOUT THE AUTHOR

Dr. Perry Daneshgari

Dr. Perry Daneshgari is president of MCA, Inc. He helps various industries improve productivity and profitability. His achievements include:

- International consulting on engineering, manufacturing, and process control to improve inventory turns and design of process flow in order to reduce companies' work-in-process inventory, waste, and production costs, and to control change.
- Consulting for various construction companies as well as distribution, automotive, manufacturing, medical, banking, and insurance organizations to improve productivity of labor, accounting, project management, estimation, and patient care.

Daneshgari is currently an adjunct professor at the University of Michigan–Dearborn and teaches master's degree courses on process and product development to engineering students. He left his full-time position as an engineering professor at the University of Michigan–Flint in 1998 to increase his activities in helping the industry.

ABOUT MCA, INC.

Dr. Perry Daneshgari created MCA, Inc. in 1990 with services focused on implementing process and product development; waste reduction; and productivity improvement of labor, project management, estimation, accounting, and customer care. Some of the industries that have benefited from his expertise are distribution, construction (electrical, mechanical, and general contractors), banking, automotive (product development and manufacturing), medical, health care, and insurance organizations.

MCA, Inc. operates as a business implementation and execution company—helping companies implement and execute improved processes. The company's implementation services go far beyond the traditional consulting role of providing advice; the company walks clients through step-by-step customized solutions.

MCA, Inc. works with various national and international companies of all sizes and industries throughout the world. Areas of specialization include: Strategic Planning, Risk Management, Productivity, Total Quality Management, Management Techniques, Cost and Risk Analysis, Facility Planning, Manufacturing, Lean/Agile Engineering and Business, and Automotive Performance.

363 East Grand Blanc Road
Grand Blanc, MI 48439
info@mca.net
Voice: 810.232.9797
Fax: 810.232.9746

www.mca.net
www.mca-soft.com

Made in the USA
Lexington, KY
12 April 2018